kids
CLOTHES
SEW EASY

Al

*I dedicate this book to the memory of my mother,
the late Eunice Duffett.*

NEW
HOLLAND

rene bergh

PHOTOGRAPHY BY WARREN HEATH

AUTHOR'S ACKNOWLEDGEMENTS

My sincere thanks go to the Struik publishing team: Linda de Villiers, Petal Palmer, Joy Clack and Bev Dodd for all the hard work that went into this wonderfully designed book; to Sean Robertson and Dave Snook for their beautiful illustrations; to Sylvie Hurford and Warren Heath for their professionalism, endless patience and bright ideas for the photography. A special thanks to all the models: Amy Dodd, April Clough, Christopher Spence Lord, Daniel and Aaron, Gabi and Jarred, Justin Fox, Mumtaaz and Ilhaam Ebrahim, Nicholas Latimer, Tara and Rochelle Dunlop, Toby Mamanzi, and Zolani Magwaxaza. And finally, to my sons, Justin and Hayden, thank you for your encouragement and for inspiring me to write this book.

This edition first published in 2003 by New Holland Publishers (UK) Ltd
London • Cape Town • Sydney • Auckland
www.newhollandpublishers.com

Garfield House, 86-88 Edgware Road
London W2 2EA, United Kingdom

80 McKenzie Street
Cape Town 8001, South Africa

Level 1, Unit 4, Suite 411, 14 Aquatic Drive
Frenchs Forest, NSW 2086, Australia

218 Lake Road, Northcote
Auckland, New Zealand

10 9 8 7 6 5 4 3 2 1

PUBLISHING MANAGER: Linda de Villiers
SENIOR DESIGNER: Petal Palmer
EDITOR: Joy Clack
DESIGNER: Beverley Dodd
PHOTOGRAPHER: Warren Heath
STYLIST: Sylvie Hurford
ILLUSTRATORS: Sean Robertson and Dave Snook

Reproduction by Hirt & Carter Cape (Pty) Ltd
Printed and bound by Sing Cheong Printing Company Limited

ISBN 1 86872 793 9

contents

introduction

Making clothes for your children can be very satisfying. From constructing the pattern, selecting the fabric and sewing the garment to seeing the end product, your very own creation, it is so worthwhile. The advantages are endless!

Kids' Clothes Sew Easy has been written for the aspirant seamstress who would like to make up simple but trendy clothes for her young ones between the ages of three and 12 years (98–152 cm/3 ft 2½ in–5 ft in height). A fundamental knowledge of sewing is advisable, though not a prerequisite. With the emphasis on simplicity, and with step-by-step instructions, this book will guide you through each stage, from conception to completion.

Bear in mind that for children, body measurements are related to height, and the ages given should only be used as a guide. Instructions are given on how to take these body measurements accurately and on how to use them to construct the essential basic patterns. These in turn are used to construct most of the basic garments.

Each chapter starts with pattern instructions, followed by sewing instructions, and offers inspirational ideas on trimmings. This is where your creativity comes into play. The garments discussed are classic, comfortable and worn by all children at some stage of their lives.

Whether you're a mum, a gran or a friend of the parent, whether you need to save a buck or just enjoy sewing for your child, you will benefit from this book by applying a few simple skills to create any number of fashionable, yet comfortable garments.

tools of the trade

Rulers

Pattern cardboard

Stapler

Safety

Square

Spiky tracing wheel

Thread clipper

Tailor's chalk

Thimbles

Awl

Spiky tracing whe

Pattern notcher

Most tools required for pattern-making and sewing can be bought from stationers, haberdasheries or sewing machine dealers. A comprehensive sewing kit will certainly speed up the process, although the bare essentials will suffice. Apart from the selection pictured here, you will also need sticky tape, marking pens, brown paper or pattern cardboard, fabric glue, pinking shears, a set square, thread, needle threader, rotary cutter, sleeve board, steam iron, pressing cloth, and, of course, a sewing machine and overlocker.

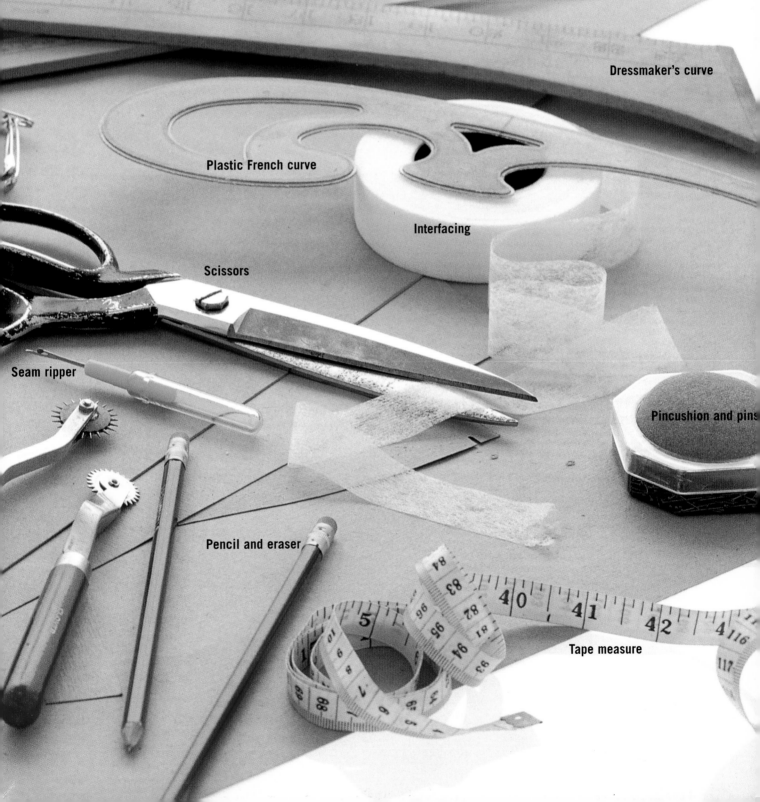

Dressmaker's curve

Plastic French curve

Interfacing

Scissors

Seam ripper

Pincushion and pins

Pencil and eraser

Tape measure

measurements

When measuring a child, hold the tape measure snugly, but not tightly, around the body. The child should wear underwear and stand in a relaxed, natural position. Bear in mind that the amount of ease added for movement and comfort, as well as the garment's style, will affect the fit. When in doubt, choose the larger measurement or size as the garment can always be taken in or worn later.

Age is not a reliable size factor as every child's body changes shape in different ways. Up to about eight years, boys and girls develop similarly. Thereafter, their shapes become more distinct. For this reason we have worked in height groups, which may alter depending on the garment. Measure your child's height before starting any pattern-making.

how to measure

Always measure around the fullest part of the chest and hips. As most children do not have a distinct waistline, tie a string around the mid-section and have the child move and bend. The string will settle on the natural waistline. To locate the neck bone for measuring the back waist length, bend the child's head forward, then tie string loosely around the neck to determine the neckline. The shoulder width is measured from the neck base, on the neckline directly below the earlobe, to the shoulder joint (found by raising the arm and feeling the indentation at the socket). Measure the overarm length from this shoulder joint, around the bent elbow, down to the wrist bone. Most length measurements will be determined by the current trends.

MEASUREMENTS REQUIRED

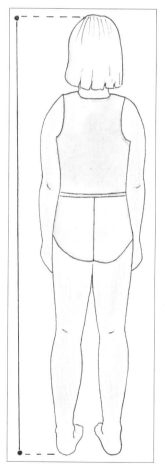

HEIGHT

From the top of the head to the floor.

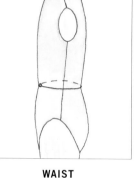

WAIST

A fairly snug measurement around the waist.

CHEST

Around the fullest part of the chest – about 5 cm (2 in) below the armhole.

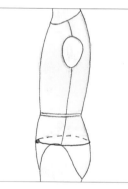

HIP

Around the fullest part of the hips – about 18 cm (7 in) below the waist.

NECK

A fairly loose measurement around the base of the neck.

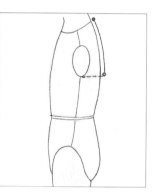

ARMHOLE DEPTH

From the nape to a line touching the base of the armhole.

WRIST

A fairly loose measurement around the wrist.

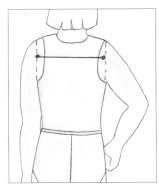

ACROSS BACK

From armhole to armhole.

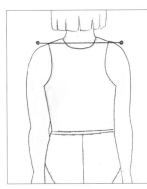

SHOULDER BREADTH

From shoulder joint to
shoulder joint.

SINGLE SHOULDER

From the neck base to
the shoulder joint.

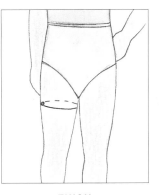

THIGH

Around the fullest part
of the thigh.

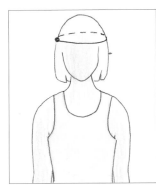

HEAD CIRCUMFERENCE

A fairly loose measurement
around the widest part of
the head.

NAPE TO WRIST

From the nape of the neck,
down the arm to the wrist.

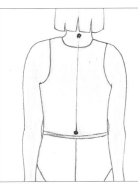

NAPE TO WAIST

From the nape of the
neck to the waist.

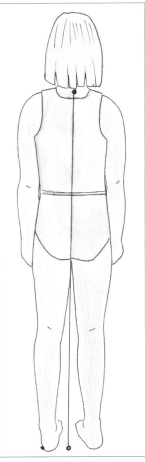

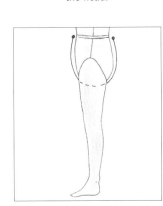

CROTCH (CF TO CB)

From the front waist through
the legs to the back waist.

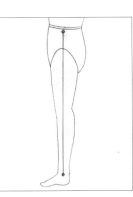

OUTSIDE LEG

From the waist, over the
hip to the ankle.

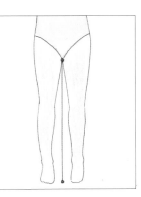

INSIDE LEG

From the crotch to the
inside of the ankle.

NAPE TO FLOOR

From the nape of the
neck to the floor.

standard measurement chart (in centimetres)

Use this as a guide to measure your child.

AGE (YEARS)	BOYS AND GIRLS						BOYS		GIRLS	
	3	4	5	6	7	8	9–10	11–12	9–10	11–12
Height	98	104	110	116	122	128	140	152	140	152
Chest	55	57	59	61	63	66	72	78	73	81
Waist	53	54	55	56	59	61	65	69	62	64
Hip	60	62	64	66	69	72	75	82	79	85
Thigh	32	33.5	35	36	38	40	46	50	44	48
Neck	27	28	29	30	31	32	34	36	34	36
Shoulder breadth	24	25	26	27	28	29	32	34	31	33
Single shoulder	7.6	8	8.4	8.8	9.2	9.6	11	12	10	10.8
Bicep	18	18.6	19.2	19.8	20.6	21.4	23	25	23	24.6
Wrist	12	12.3	12.6	12.9	13.2	13.5	14.5	15.5	14.2	15
Armhole depth	12.7	13.4	14.1	14.8	15.5	16.2	17.4	18.6	17.4	18.6
Nape to wrist	45	48.5	52	55.5	59	62	66	71	66	71
Nape to waist	23.3	24.6	25.9	27.2	28.5	29.8	33	36	32.5	35.5
Nape to floor	81	86	91	96	101	107	118	129	118	129
Outside leg	58	62	66	70	75	80	88	96	88	96
Inside leg	40.5	44	47.5	51	54.5	58	63	69	64	70
Knee height	25	27	29	31	32.5	34	40	43	40	43
Crotch (CF to CB)	43.5	45	47.5	50	52.5	55	60	63	60	63
Head circumference	50.5	50.8	51.1	51.4	51.9	52.4	55.3	56.5	52.8	54

imperial conversion (in inches) of standard measurement chart

	BOYS AND GIRLS						BOYS		GIRLS	
AGE (YEARS)	**3**	**4**	**5**	**6**	**7**	**8**	**9–10**	**11–12**	**9–10**	**11–12**
Height	3' 2½"	3' 5"	3' 7"	3' 9½"	4'	4' 2½"	4' 7"	5'	4' 7"	5'
Chest	21½	22½	23¼	24	24¾	26	28¼	30¾	28¾	32
Waist	21	21¼	21½	22	23¼	24	25½	27	24½	25
Hip	23½	24½	25	26	27	28¼	29½	32¼	31	33½
Thigh	12½	13¼	13¾	14	15	15¾	18	19½	17½	19
Neck	10¾	11	11½	11¾	12¼	12½	13½	14¼	13½	14¼
Shoulder breadth	9½	9¾	10¼	10¾	11	11½	12½	13½	12¼	13
Single shoulder	3	3⅛	33¼	3⅜	3½	3¾	4¼	4¾	4	4¼
Bicep	7	7¼	7½	7¾	8	8½	9	10	9	9¾
Wrist	4¾	4⅞	5	5⅛	5¼	5⅜	5¾	6⅛	5⅝	5⅞
Armhole depth	5	5¼	5½	5⅞	6⅛	6⅜	6⅞	7⅜	6⅞	7⅜
Nape to wrist	17¾	19	20½	22	23¼	24½	26	28	26	28
Nape to waist	9⅛	9¾	10¼	10¾	11¼	11¾	13	14¼	12¾	14
Nape to floor	32	34	36	37¾	39¾	42	46½	50¾	46½	50¾
Outside leg	23	24½	26	27½	29½	31½	34½	37¾	34½	37¾
Inside leg	16	17½	18¾	20	21½	23	24¾	27	25	27½
Knee height	9¾	10¾	11½	12½	12¾	13½	15¾	17	15¾	17
Crotch (CF to CB)	17¼	17¾	18¾	19¾	20¾	21¾	23½	24¾	23½	24¾
Head circumference	19⅞	20	20⅛	20¼	20½	20¾	21¾	22¼	20⅞	21¼

basic blocks

Pattern-drafting is a way of making patterns, by working from figure measurements according to a set of instructions and drawing the outline on paper. These basic patterns are known as 'blocks'. They provide a permanent record of the correct fit and are easily adapted to create almost any style. A perfect fit is essential, and blocks are made without seam allowances to facilitate any alterations. Seam allowances can be added to the final pattern. Blocks are not intended for use as patterns, i.e. for cutting out fabric, except when cutting a calico model to check the fit. Fold out the centre front and centre back patterns to check that the neckline is correctly curved, and match shoulder seams to round off the top of the armhole.

the bodice

This bodice block is for pre-school boys and girls from height 98–122 cm (3 ft 2½ in–4 ft) and girls from height 128–152 cm (4 ft 2 in–5 ft). Where the measurements in construction differ between these two groups, we will refer to the former as children's size and the latter as girls' size. The blocks include a basic amount of ease required for the use of the block. No seams have been added. For beginners, it is easier to work with these net patterns, especially when new designs are developed. Seam allowances of 1 cm (⅜ in) should be added to all seams when the final pattern adaptation is complete.

Measurements required: chest, across back, neck circumference, single shoulder, nape to waist and armhole depth (refer to pages 10–11).

BASIC BODICE

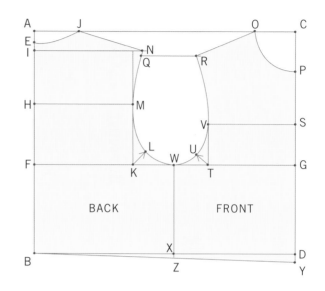

AB	=	Nape to waist plus 1.25 cm (½ in). Draw vertical line.
AC	=	½ chest plus 4 cm (1⅝ in) for children's size, or plus 4.5 cm (1¾ in) for girls' size. Square a line across from A to C.
CD	=	Square a line down from C.
BD	=	Square a line across from B.
AE	=	1.25 cm (½ in).
EF	=	Armhole depth plus 1 cm (⅜ in). Square a line across to G.
EH	=	½ EF. Square a line across from H.
EI	=	¼ armhole depth minus 2 cm (¾ in). Square a line across from I.
AJ	=	⅕ neck circumference minus 0.2 cm (¹⁄₁₆ in). Draw neck curve.
FK	=	½ across back plus 0.5 cm (³⁄₁₆ in). Square a line up from K. Mark M. HM = FK.
KL	=	2 cm (¾ in) for children's size, or 2.25 cm (⅞ in) for girls' size. Draw a diagonal line to L.

Denim jeans worn with a T-shirt and zipped sweatshirt.

basic blocks

JN	=	Single shoulder measurement plus 0.3 cm (⅛ in) ease for children's size, or 0.5 cm (³⁄₁₆ in) ease for girls' size. Draw back shoulder line to touch line from I.
CO	=	⅕ neck circumference minus 0.5 cm (³⁄₁₆ in).
CP	=	⅕ neck circumference minus 0.2 cm (¹⁄₁₆ in). Draw neck curve.
NQ	=	0.5 cm (³⁄₁₆ in). Square a line across from Q.
OR	=	Shoulder measurement. Draw front shoulder line to touch line from Q.
PS	=	½ GP plus 1 cm (⅜ in) for children's size, or plus 1.5 cm (⅝ in) for girls' size. Square a line across from S.
GT	=	FK minus 1 cm (⅜ in) for children's size, or minus 0.75 cm (¼ in) for girls' size. Square a line up from T. Mark V. SV = GT.
TU	=	1.75 cm (⅝ in) for children's size, or 2 cm (¾ in) for girls' size. Draw a diagonal line to U.
TW	=	½ KT plus 0.5 cm (³⁄₁₆ in). Square a line down from W to X.
DY	=	1.5 cm (⅝ in) for children's size, or 1 cm (⅜ in) for girls' size. Join BY, curving slightly as illustrated. Extend WX to cross BY at Z.

Draw in armhole from N to M to L to W to U to V to R.
Cut out back bodice along B, E, J, N, W, Z, B.
Cut out front bodice along Z, Y, P, O, R, W.

SHAPING THE BODICE

The bodice may require shaping at the waist for some designs. Waist shaping without darts is suitable up to a height of 122 cm (4 ft), but darts must be added for larger sizes. For this purpose, these larger sizes have been broken down into group 1, height 116–122 cm (3 ft 10 in–4 ft); group 2, height 128–134 cm (4 ft 2 in–4 ft 5 in); and group 3, height 140–152 cm (4 ft 7 in–5 ft).

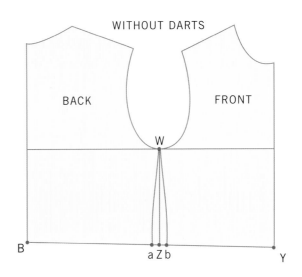

Use basic bodice block without seams.

Ba	=	¼ waist plus 1.25 cm (½ in).
Yb	=	¼ waist plus 1.75 cm (⅝ in).

Curve Wa and Wb slightly as illustrated.
Adjust side seam so that Wa = Wb.

- The grainlines on bodices and skirts are along the CF and CB seams, perpendicular to the hems. On trousers, sleeves and panels, the grainlines are centrally positioned, perpendicular to the hem.
- Notch matching seams at strategic positions.

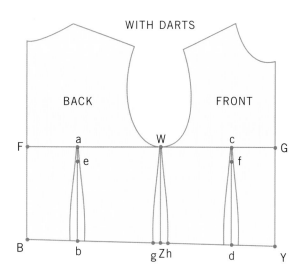

WITH DARTS

BACK   FRONT

the sleeve

Measurements required: armhole depth and sleeve length (refer to pages 11–12).

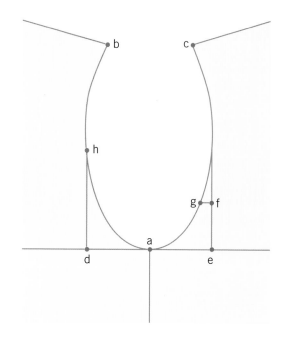

Use basic bodice block without seams.

Fa = ½ FK.

Square a line down from a to b.

Gc = ½ GT.

Square a line down from c to d.

ae = 2 cm (¾ in).

cf = 2 cm (¾ in).

Bg = ¼ waist

plus 1.75 cm (⅝ in) for group 1,

plus 2.25 cm (⅞ in) for group 2,

plus 2.75 cm (1⅛ in) for group 3.

Yh = ¼ waist

plus 2.25 cm (⅞ in) for group 1,

plus 2.75 cm (1⅛ in) for group 2,

plus 3.75 cm (1½ in) for group 3.

Curve Wg and Wh slightly as illustrated.

Mark back and front darts on lines eb and fd:

0.5 cm (³⁄₁₆ in) both darts for group 1,

1 cm (⅜ in) both darts for group 2,

1.5 cm (⅝ in) back dart for group 3,

2 cm (¾ in) front dart for group 3.

Adjust side seam so that Wg = Wh.

Align back and front basic bodice blocks at side seams.
Trace outline of armhole as illustrated.

Mark point a at underarm, b at back shoulder and c at front shoulder.

Mark armhole depth line through a, perpendicular to side seam.

Square up from d and e on armhole depth line to touch back and front armholes.

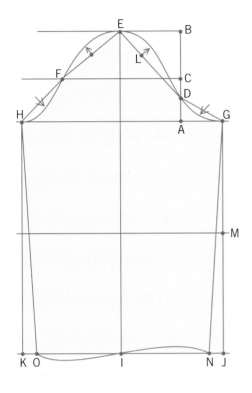

Square a line up and across from A.

AB = ⅓ armhole depth plus 0.25 cm (⅟₁₆ in).
Square a line across from B.

AC = ½ AB.
Square a line across from C.

AD = ½ AC.

ON BODY BLOCK

ef = AD on sleeve block.
Square across to g on front armhole.

dh = AC on sleeve block.

ON SLEEVE BLOCK

DE = cg measured in a curve
plus 0.5 cm (³⁄₁₆ in) for children's size,
or plus 0.75 cm (¼ in) for girls' size.
Join DE.

EF = bh measured in a curve
plus 0.5 cm (³⁄₁₆ in) for children's size,
or plus 0.75 cm (¼ in) for girls' size.
Join EF.

DG = ga measured in a curve.
Join DG.

FH = ha measured in a curve.
Join FH.

EI = overarm sleeve length.
Square across from I to J and K.

Draw sleeve crown as follows:

Hollow F to H	0.4 cm (⅛ in) for children's size, 0.5 cm (³⁄₁₆ in) for girls' size.
Raise E to F	0.8 cm (¼ in) for children's size, 1 cm (⅜ in) for girls' size.

EL = ⅓ ED. Mark L on ED.

Raise curve at L	1.4 cm (½ in) for children's size, 1.6 cm (⅝ in) for girls' size.
Hollow D to G	0.6 cm (¼ in) for children's size, 0.7 cm (⁵⁄₁₆ in) for girls' size.

Square down from G to J and H to K.

GM = ½ GJ.
Square across from M.

JN = ⅙ IJ. Mark N.

KO = ⅙ IK. Mark O.

Join GN and HO.

Lower curve on OI	0.5 cm (³⁄₁₆ in) for children's size, 0.7 cm (⁵⁄₁₆ in) for girls' size.
Raise curve on IN	0.5 cm (³⁄₁₆ in) for children's size, 0.7 cm (⁵⁄₁₆ in) for girls' size.

the skirt

The skirt block has been broken down into group 1: girls size 98–104 cm (3 ft 2½ in–3 ft 5 in) height, no darts required; group 2a: girls 110–122 cm (3 ft 7 in–4 ft) height; group 2b: girls 128–140 cm (4 ft 2 in–4 ft 7 in) height, darts added; and group 3: girls 146–152 cm (4 ft 9½ in–5 ft) height, more shapely darts added. The dartless skirt has 5 cm (2 in) ease, whereas the darted skirt has 1 cm (⅜ in) ease.

Measurements required: waist, hip, waist to hip and waist to knee (skirt length) (refer to pages 10–11).

BACK

Square a line across and down from A.

AB = skirt length plus 1 cm (⅜ in).
Square across from B.

AC = waist to hip plus 1 cm (⅜ in).
Square across from C.

CD = ¼ hip plus 1.5 cm (⅝ in).
Square up to E and down to F.

AG = ¼ waist plus 1 cm (⅜ in) for group 1,
plus 1.2 cm (½ in) for group 2a,
plus 1.5 cm (⅝ in) for group 2b,
plus 2.6 cm (1 in) for group 3.

AH = 1 cm (⅜ in).
Curve GH.

FI = 2.5 cm (1 in) for groups 1, 2a and 2b,
3 cm (1¼ in) for group 3.
Draw side seam GDI, curving hipline outwards
0.25 cm (1/16 in) for groups 1, 2a and 2b,
0.4 cm (⅛ in) for group 3.
Curve hem up 0.25 cm (1/16 in) at I, as shown.

Dartless back is complete for group 1.

FOR GROUPS 2A AND 2B:

S = ½ HE.
Square down from S.

Dart = 1 cm (⅜ in) width, 8 cm (3⅛ in) length for group 2a,
1.5 cm (⅝ in) width, 9 cm (3½ in) length for group 2b.

FOR GROUP 3:

Divide HG into three so that HU = UW = WG.
Square down from U and W.

Dart UV = 1.2 cm (½ in) width, 10 cm (4 in) length.
Dart WX = 1.2 cm (½ in) width, 8 cm (3⅛ in) length.

GROUP 1

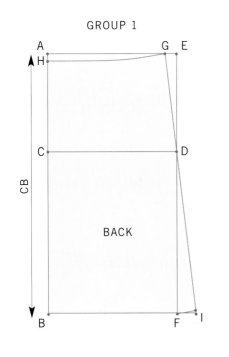

GROUPS 2A AND 2B

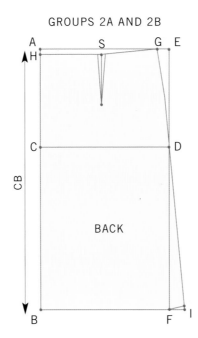

GROUP 3

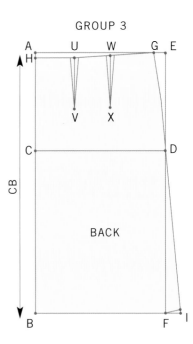

basic blocks

FRONT

Square a line across and down from J.

JK = skirt length plus 1 cm (⅜ in).
Square across from K.

JL = Waist to hip plus 1 cm (⅜ in).
Square across from L.

LM = ¼ hip
plus 2 cm (¾ in) for group 1,
plus 1.5 cm (⅝ in) for groups
2a and 2b,
plus 1 cm (⅜ in) for group 3.
Square up to N and down to O.

JP = ¼ waist
plus 1.5 cm (⅝ in) for group 1,
plus 1.3 cm (½ in) for group 2a,
plus 1.8 cm (¾ in) for groups 2b and 3.

JQ = 0.5 cm (³⁄₁₆ in) for groups 1, 2a and 2b,
1 cm (⅜ in) for group 3.
Curve PQ.

OR = 2.5 cm (1 in) for groups 1, 2a and 2b,
3 cm (1¼ in) for group 3.
Draw side seam PMR, curving hipline
outwards 0.25 cm (¹⁄₁₆ in).
Curve hem up 0.25 cm (¹⁄₁₆ in) at R.

Dartless front is complete for group 1.

FOR GROUPS 2A AND 2B:

T = ½ PQ.
Square down from T.

Dart = 1 cm (⅜ in) width, 6.5 cm (2½ in) length for
group 2a,
1.5 cm (⅝ in) width, 7.5 cm (3 in) length for
group 2b.

FOR GROUP 3:

PY = ½ PQ minus 2 cm (¾ in).
Square down from Y.

YZ = Dart length 8 cm (3⅛ in), width 1.5 cm (⅝ in).

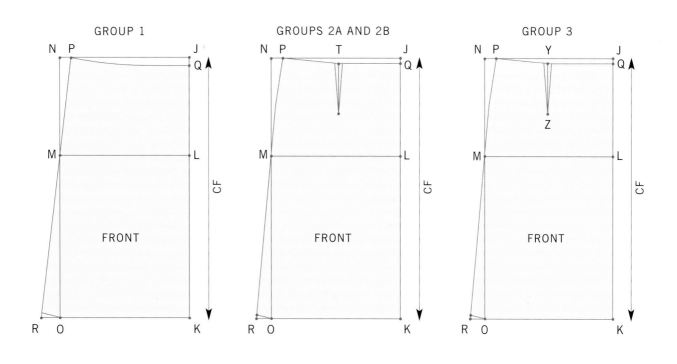

GROUP 1   GROUPS 2A AND 2B   GROUP 3

the dress

The one-piece dress block has an easy fit and slightly high-waisted shape. This allows for the rather large stomachs that small children tend to have. The back and front bodice blocks (pages 16–17) are used to construct these patterns. To maintain consistency, the dress block is knee length. Because young children stoop forwards, extra fullness is required in the front block for size 98–122 cm (3 ft 2½ in–4 ft) height.

FRONT

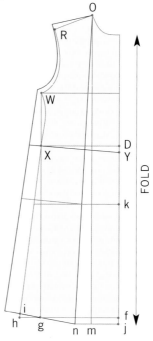

BACK

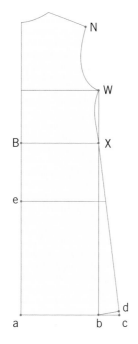

Trace around the back bodice, using BX as waistline.

Mark points B, N, W, X.

Square down from B and X.

Ba = Waist to knee.
Square across to b.

bc = 5 cm (2 in).
Join Xc.

Xd = Xb.
Curve hem slightly to d.

Curve side seam inwards by 0.75 cm (¼ in) between X and W.

Be = Waist to hip.
Square across.

Trace around the front bodice block, using the line DX as the waistline.

Mark points D, O, R, W, X.

Square down from D and X.

Df = Waist to knee.
Square across to g.

gh = 5 cm (2 in).
Join Xh.

Xi = Xg.

fj = **DY** = 1.5 cm (⅝ in) for children's size,
1 cm (⅜ in) for girls' size.
Curve hem from j to i.
Curve waistline from Y to X.

Dk = Waist to hip.
Square across.

For children's size front:

Square down from O to m.

Cut out dress front.

Cut from m to (but not through) O and spread pattern.

mn = 2.5 cm (1 in) for size 98–104 cm
(3 ft 2½ in–3 ft 5 in) height,
1.5 cm (⅝ in) for size 110–122 cm
(3 ft 7 in–4 ft) height.

Trace around new shape.

Re-mark waistline, hipline and armhole depth line slightly curved.

SLEEVELESS DRESS

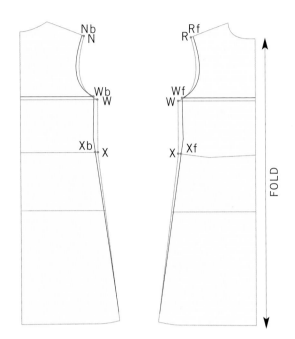

Trace outline of back and front dress blocks.

Mark N, W, X on back and R, W, X on front.

Raise armhole depth 1 cm (⅜ in).

Reduce armhole by 1 cm (⅜ in).

Mark Wb on back and Wf on front.

Reduce shoulder length by 0.75 cm (¼ in).

Mark Nb on back shoulder and Rf on front shoulder.

Reduce waist by 0.75 cm (¼ in).

Mark Xb on back and Xf on front.

Draw in new reduced shape for back from Nb to Wb to Xb to original side seam at the hem.

Draw in new reduced shape for front from Rf to Wf to Xf to original side seam at the hem.

Dress with high-cut bodice and short, cap sleeves.

the trouser

The top of the waistband for children up to height 122 cm (4 ft) and all boys sits on the waistline; for taller girls, the bottom of the waistband sits on the waistline. For the trouser construction, we will refer to children's size 98–122 cm (3 ft 2½ in–4 ft) height as group 1; all boys' size 98–152 cm (3 ft 2½ in–5 ft) height as group 2; girls' size 128–140 cm (4 ft 2 in–4 ft 7 in) height as group 3; and girls' size 146–152 cm (4 ft 9½ in–5 ft) height as group 4.

Measurements required: hip, waist, crotch, inside leg, trouser bottom width, waist to hip and waistband width (refer to pages 10–11).

FRONT

Square down and across from A.

AB = Crotch plus 1 cm (⅜ in), minus waistband width for groups 1 and 2.
Crotch for groups 3 and 4.
Square across.

AC = Waist to hip plus 1 cm (⅜ in), minus waistband width for groups 1 and 2.
Waist to hip for groups 3 and 4.
Square across.

BD = Inside leg.
Square across.

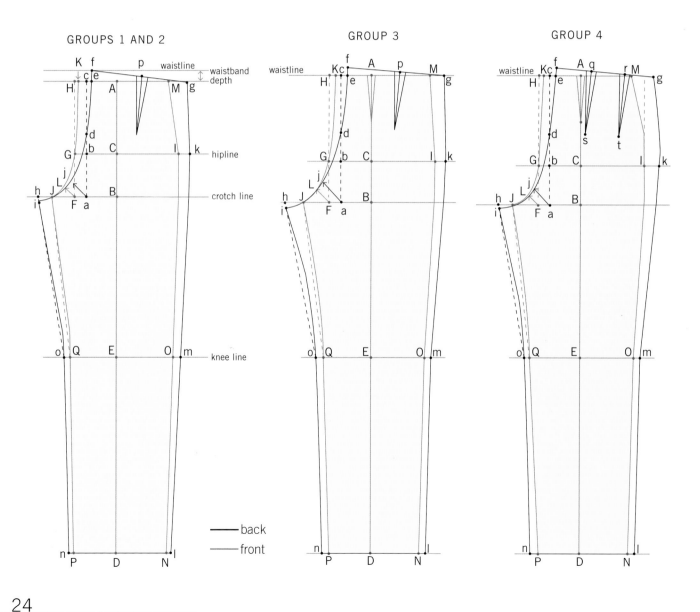

GROUPS 1 AND 2   GROUP 3   GROUP 4

back
front

BE = ½ BD

minus 3 cm (1¼ in) for group 1,

minus 3.5 cm (1⅜ in) for groups 2 and 3,

minus 4 cm (1⅝ in) for group 4.

Square across.

BF = $\frac{1}{12}$ hip plus 1.5 cm (⅝ in).

Square up to G and H.

GI = ¼ hip

plus 1.5 cm (⅝ in) for group 1,

plus 1 cm (⅜ in) for groups 2 and 3,

plus 0.5 cm (³⁄₁₆ in) for group 4.

Square up for group 4 only.

FJ = $\frac{1}{16}$ hip plus 0.5 cm (³⁄₁₆ in).

HK = 1 cm (⅜ in).

Join KG.

FL = 2.25 cm (⅞ in) for group 1,

2.5 cm (1 in) for groups 2 and 3,

2.75 cm (1⅛ in) for group 4.

Draw a diagonal line to L.

Curve G, L, J to mark front crotch.

KM = ¼ waist

plus 0.75 cm (¼ in) for group 1,

plus 0.25 cm (⅛ in) for group 2,

plus 1.25 cm (½ in) for group 3,

plus 1.6 cm (⅝ in) for group 4.

DN = **DP** = ½ bottom width minus 0.5 cm (³⁄₁₆ in).

EO = **EQ** = DN plus 1 cm (⅜ in).

Draw outside leg M, I, O, N, curving MI outwards 0.25 cm (⅛ in).

Draw inside leg J, Q, P, curving JQ inwards 0.75 cm (¼ in).

Trouser front is complete for groups 1 and 2.

FOR GROUPS 3 AND 4:

Mark dart on AC.

Dart = 1 cm (⅜ in) width, 8 cm (3⅛ in) length for group 3,

1.4 cm (⅝ in) width, 7.5 cm (3 in) length for group 4.

Trace outline of front trouser block.

BACK

Continue on front trouser construction.

Fa = ¼ FB.

Square up to b on GI/hip and c on HM/waist.

ad = ½ ac.

ce = **ef** = 1.5 cm (⅝ in).

fg = ¼ waist

plus 1.25 cm (½ in) for group 1,

plus 2.25 cm (⅞ in) for groups 2 and 3,

plus 2.7 cm (1 in) for group 4.

Mark fg to touch horizontal line from A.

Jh = ½ FJ.

hi = 0.25 cm (⅛ in).

aj = 3.5 cm (1⅜ in) for group 1,

3.75 cm (1½ in) for groups 2 and 3,

4 cm (1⅝ in) for group 4.

Draw a diagonal line to j.

Curve f, e, d, j, i to mark back crotch.

bk = ¼ hip

plus 1 cm (⅜ in) for group 1,

plus 1.25 cm (½ in) for groups 2, 3 and 4.

NI = **Pn** = 1 cm (⅜ in).

Om = **Qo** = 1 cm (⅜ in).

Draw outside leg g, k, m, l, curving gk outwards 0.25 cm (⅛ in), curving km inwards 0.25 cm (⅛ in).

Draw inside leg i, o, n, curving io inwards 1.25 cm (½ in).

FOR GROUPS 1, 2 AND 3:

fp = ½ fg.

Square down from p.

Dart = 1.5 cm (⅝ in) width, 7.5 cm (3 in) length for group 1,

2 cm (¾ in) width, 9 cm (3½ in) length for groups 2 and 3.

FOR GROUP 4:

Divide fg into three so that fq = qr = rg.

Square down from q and r.

Dart qs = 1.2 cm (½ in) width, 10 cm (4 in) length.

Dart rt = 1.2 cm (½ in) width, 8 cm (3⅛ in) length.

t-shirts

The T-shirt is a comfortable garment; it wears well and is very versatile. It is probably the most popular garment worn by children worldwide, and it can easily withstand the wear and tear of active play. The shape and fit may vary from season to season; it could be tighter for girls and looser for boys, but the basic T-shirt is here to stay. The necklines can be round, boat-necked or V-necked. They can be trimmed with ribbing or bound in self- or contrast fabric; some have facings to complement the shape of the neck. T-shirts can be sleeveless or have short or long sleeves; some sleeves may even be layered. These garments are simple to make and can be easily embellished to create the season's latest style.

t-shirt pattern

This T-shirt pattern is made for knitted fabrics and has an easy fit, but it is not an oversized, loose T-shirt. The back, chest and armhole depth measurements will need to be increased to aquire a baggy shape. The sizes for the T-shirt construction will be referred to as group 1, for size 98–134 cm (3 ft 2½ in–4 ft 5 in) height and group 2, for size 140–152 cm (4 ft 7 in–5 ft) height.

MEASUREMENTS REQUIRED

CHEST

ACROSS BACK

NAPE TO WAIST

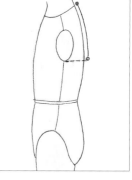

ARMHOLE DEPTH

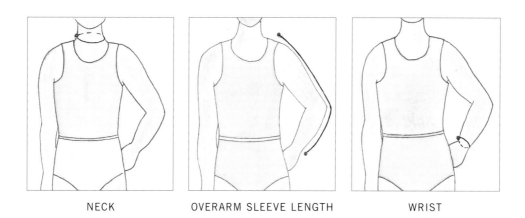

NECK

OVERARM SLEEVE LENGTH

WRIST

BACK AND FRONT

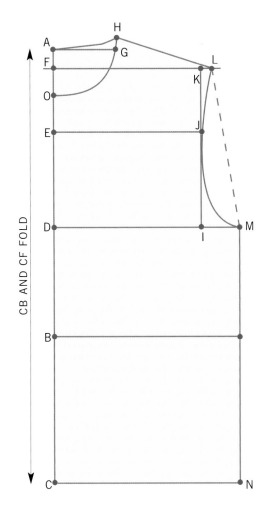

CB AND CF FOLD

- Back and front sections are the same except for the necklines.
- Cut the centre front and centre back on the fold.

Square down and across from A.

AB	=	Neck to waist.
		Square across from B.
AC	=	Finished length of centre back.
		Square across from C.
AD	=	Armhole depth
		plus 0.5 cm (³⁄₁₆ in) for group 1,
		plus 1 cm (⅜ in) for group 2.
		Square across.
AE	=	½ AD.
		Square across.
AF	=	¼ AE.
		Square across.
AG	=	⅕ neck circumference plus 0.25 cm (⅛ in).
		Square up from G.
GH	=	1.25 cm (½ in) for group 1,
		1.5 cm (⅝ in) for group 2.
		Draw back neck curve.
DI	=	½ across back.
		Square up to J and K.
KL	=	0.5 cm (³⁄₁₆ in).
		Join HL.
DM	=	¼ chest
		plus 1 cm (⅜ in) for group 1,
		plus 1.5 cm (⅝ in) for group 2.
		Square down to N.

Draw in armhole from L to J to M.

AO	=	⅕ neck circumference minus 1 cm (⅜ in).

Draw front neck curve.

SLEEVE

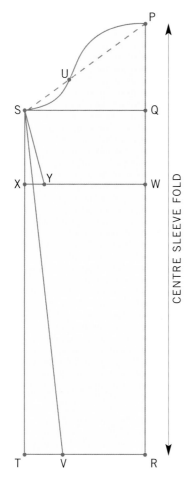

CENTRE SLEEVE FOLD

PR = Overarm long sleeve length.
Square across from R.

PQ = ½ armhole depth plus 1 cm (⅜ in).
Square across from Q.

PS = Diagonal line LM on back/front pattern
plus 2 cm (¾ in).
Mark S on line from Q.
Square down to T.

SU = ⅓ SP

Draw sleeve crown as follows:

Hollow S to U   0.4 cm (⅛ in) for group 1,
                          0.6 cm (¼ in) for group 2.

Raise U to P   1.25 cm (½ in) for group 1,
                          1.75 cm (¾ in) for group 2.

FOR LONG SLEEVE:

RV = ½ wrist
plus 1.5 cm (⅝ in) for group 1,
plus 2 cm (¾ in) for group 2.
Join SV.

FOR SHORT SLEEVE:

PW = Overarm short sleeve length.
Square across from W.

XY = 2.25 cm (⅞ in) for group 1,
2.5 cm (1 in) for group 2.
Join SY.

RAGLAN CONVERSION

A raglan sleeve allows for greater freedom of movement.
It is most suitable for fast-growing children, but can also
be used as a design detail.

BACK AND FRONT

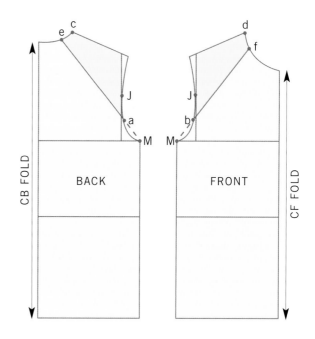

Trace back and front pattern separately.

aM = **bM** = SU on sleeve.

Curve line inwards   1 cm (⅜ in) for group 1,

                         1.5 cm (⅝ in) for group 2.

ec = **df** = 2 cm (¾ in) for 98–122 cm (3 ft

                      2½ in–4 ft),

                      2.5 cm (1 in) for 128–152 cm

                      (4 ft 2 in–5 ft).

Join ae and bf.

SLEEVE

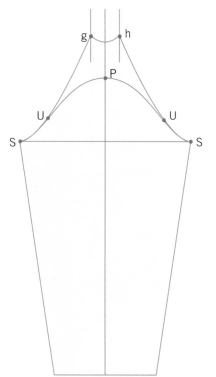

Trace sleeve pattern.

Extend centre line of sleeve.

Draw parallel lines on either side of the centre line, measuring:

    2 cm (¾ in) for 98–122 cm (3 ft 2½ in–4 ft)
    height,

    2.5 cm (1 in) for 128–152 cm (4 ft 2 in–5 ft)
    height.

Ug = ae on back.

Uh = bf on front.

Join gh with a curve.

- Add 1 cm (⅜ in) seams all round.
- Position notches at strategic matching points.
- For mock safety stitch, add 6 mm (¼ in) all round.
- Add 2 cm (¾ in) for hems.
- No seams required for neck, if bound.
- For ribbed neck, trim away width of rib from neck.
- For faced neck, make the facings 3–5 cm (1¼–2 in) wide.

fabric suggestions

T-shirts are usually cut in single jersey or double knit. Cotton knit is comfortable to wear because this fibre is absorbent and breathes. Follow care instructions closely as these fabrics may shrink, fade and crease unless special manufacturing finishes have been applied. Polyester cotton blends are easy to care for; their colours are permanent and they are crease resistant.

Single-jersey fabric is available in a multitude of colours.

to sew

1 Select a suitable cotton knit fabric, matching rib and interfacing if required.

2 Lay up the fabric and cut out the T-shirt, following the grain lines very carefully. Fuse any interfacings.

3 Join the shoulder seams and overlock the edges. If very stretchy fabric is going to be used, insert tape or a strip of self-fabric (cut lengthwise) when overlocking to prevent the seam from stretching out. Press the seams towards the back.

4 Join the edges of the neck ribbing using 6 mm (¼ in) seams. Fold in half lengthwise, with wrong sides facing, and divide into four equal parts. Mark with pins. Place a pin at the centre front and divide the neck into fourths from that point, marking with pins.

5 Position the ribbing seam at the left shoulder and match the pin markers of the ribbing to those of the neck. With the ribbing on top, stitch a 6 mm (¼ in) seam using an overedge stretch stitch, narrow zigzag or overlock. Stretch the ribbing to fit the garment neck between the pins. Press the seam towards the garment.

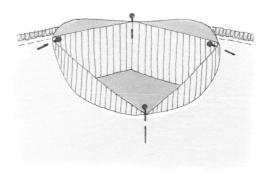

6 For a professional-looking finish, bind the back neck, from shoulder to shoulder, encasing the seam allowances in the binding. Topstitch the neck seams.

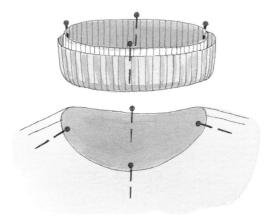

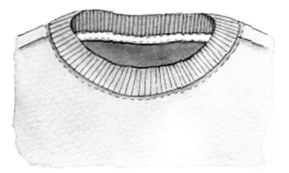

7 Attach any pockets, motifs or inserts at this stage, if required. With right sides facing, match and pin the sleeve to the armhole, aligning the notches. Stitch with the sleeve side up.

8 If topstitching or any other decorative stitching is required around the armhole, overlock the edges, press the seam allowances towards the garment and, with right side up, stitch as required. If no topstitching is required, trim the seams to 6 mm (¼ in) with the overlocker. Press the seam towards the sleeve.

9 With right sides facing, match and pin the underarm seams. Stitch one continuous seam from the hem of the garment to the hem of the sleeve. Trim the seam allowances to 6 mm (¼ in) when overlocking. Overlock the edges and stitch the hems of the sleeve and the body. Trim off all unwanted threads and press.

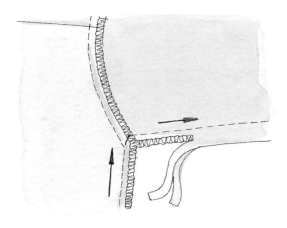

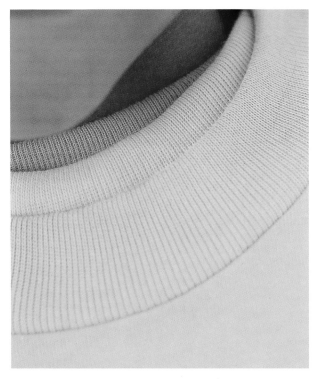

One-by-one ribbing is usually used for the neck of a T-shirt.

embellishing

There is so much scope for restyling the basic T-shirt. Depending on current trends, you can paint your own design on the T-shirt, add embroidery, tie-dye the garment, stick on sequins, fringe the hem and thread beads on the fringes, knot the hem or sleeves – the ideas are endless. Insert or stitch on printed panels to co-ordinate with shorts, add collars or pockets, layer sleeves or hems, colour block by cutting panels, contrast sleeves and body, cut double fronts with different necklines – there are an infinite number of styles to create. Be an individualist and design your own garment.

tracksuits

This two-piece outfit was originally worn only by athletes but became a fashion item in the 1970s. The long-sleeved sweatshirt can be trimmed with ribbing at the neck, cuffs and hem, it may have a drawstring or elasticated waist, or it may have no trim at all.

Track pants are usually elasticated at the waist and hem, but are often trimmed with a ribbed cuff at the ankle. Children of all ages love wearing tracksuits. They are warm and comfortable and so functional that many schools have adapted them into a uniform.

Knits or wovens can be used, unlined or lined for extra warmth, and the trimming options are boundless. Tracksuits are simple to sew, easy for play and here to stay!

tracksuit pattern

This tracksuit pattern, consisting of a sweatshirt and track pants, has a standard fit and has been drafted for knitted fabrics. For the sweatshirt, similar instructions are given to that of the T-shirt, and the crotch on the pants has been increased to allow for an easier fit. Increased measurements are required for a looser fit, but the method of construction remains the same. The sizes for this draft are as follows: 98–134 cm (3 ft 2½ in– 4 ft 5 in) for group 1 and 140–152 cm (4 ft 7 in–5 ft) for group 2.

MEASUREMENTS REQUIRED

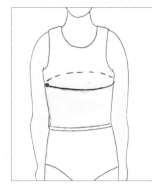 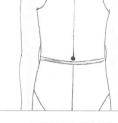  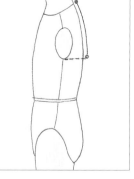

| CHEST | ACROSS BACK | NAPE TO WAIST | ARMHOLE DEPTH |

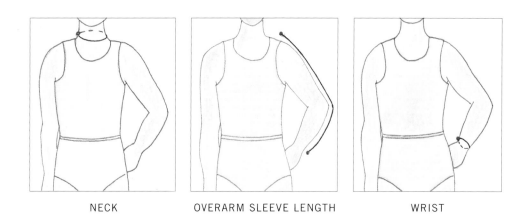

| NECK | OVERARM SLEEVE LENGTH | WRIST |

SWEATSHIRT

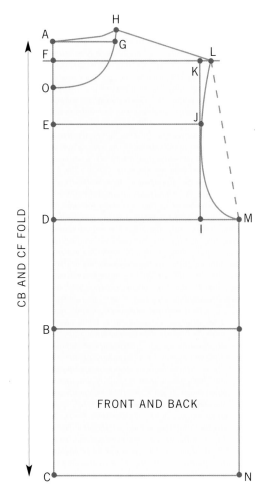

CB AND CF FOLD

FRONT AND BACK

- For faced neck, make neck facings 3–5 cm (1¼–2 in) wide.
- For ribbed neck, trim away width of rib from the neckline.
- The raglan conversion (page 30) can be used for the sweatshirt as well.

Square down and across from A.

AB	=	Neck to waist.
		Square across from B.
AC	=	Finished length of centre back.
		Square across from C.
AD	=	Armhole depth
		plus 2.5 cm (1 in) for size 98–122 cm (3 ft 2½ in–4 ft) height,
		plus 3 cm (1¼ in) for size 128–152 cm (4 ft 2 in–5 ft) height.
AE	=	½ AD.
		Square across.
AF	=	¼ AE.
		Square across.
AG	=	⅕ neck circumference plus 0.25 cm (⅛ in).
		Square up from G.
GH	=	1.25 cm (½ in) for group 1,
		1.5 cm (⅝ in) for group 2.
DI	=	½ across back plus 1.25 cm (½ in).
		Square up to J and K.
KL	=	0.75 cm (⅜ in).
		Join HL.
DM	=	¼ chest
		plus 4 cm (1⅝ in) for group 1,
		plus 4.5 cm (1¾ in) for group 2.
		Square down to N.

Draw in armhole L to J to M.

AO	=	⅕ neck circumference minus 1 cm (⅜ in).

Draw front neck curve.

SLEEVE

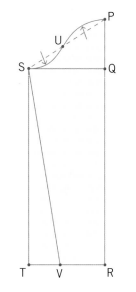

PR = Overarm long sleeve length.
Square across from R.

PQ = ½ armhole depth plus 1 cm (⅜ in).

PS = Diagonal line LM on back/front pattern plus
2 cm (¾ in).
Mark S on line from Q.
Square down to T.

SU = ⅓ SP.

Draw sleeve crown as follows:

Hollow S to U   0.4 cm (⅛ in) for group 1,
0.6 cm (¼ in) for group 2.

Raise U to P   1.25 cm (½ in) for group 1,
1.75 cm (¾ in) for group 2.

RV = Wrist
plus 2 cm (¾ in) for group 1,
plus 3 cm (1¼ in) for group 2.

Join SV.

- For elasticated cuff, add casing according
to elastic width. For ribbed cuff, remove half
width of cuff from length of sleeve.
- Add 1 cm (⅜ in) seams all round.

PANTS

Trace back and front of basic trouser block (page 24).

AB = Crotch plus 2 cm (¾ in).
Adjust block crotch.
Erase waist darts.

BACK

---- basic trouser
block

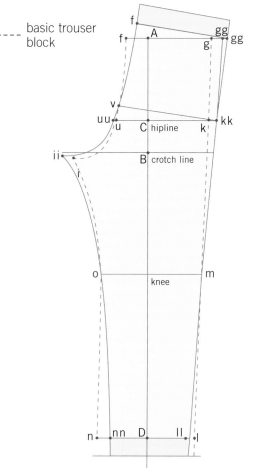

Mark u and k on hipline.

i to ii	=	1 cm (⅜ in).
g to gg	=	2 cm (¾ in) for group 1,
		2.5 cm (1 in) for group 2.
k to kk	=	1.5 cm (⅝ in) for group 1,
		2 cm (¾ in) for group 2.
n to nn = l to ll	=	1 cm (⅜ in) for group 1,
		1.5 cm (⅝ in) for group 2.

Draw inside leg ii, o, nn.

Draw side seam gg, kk, m, ll.

Holding a pencil down at kk, lengthen crotch by pivoting pattern.

uv = 2.5 cm (1 in) for group 1,
3 cm (1¼ in) for group 2.

u to uu = 0.5 cm (³⁄₁₆ in).

Draw new crotch, waist and hip ii, uu, v, f, gg, kk.

- Add 1 cm (⅜ in) seams all round.
- Add about 4 cm (1⅝ in) to waist and hem for casings.
- Instead of pivoting, slash from u to kk, and raise u by 2.5 cm (1 in)/3 cm (1¼ in) as required.
- Grainline is always central, perpendicular to hem.

FRONT

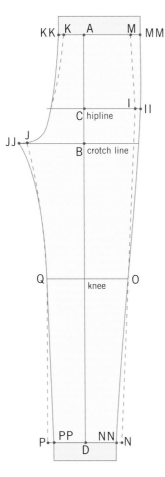

K to KK = 1 cm (⅜ in).

J to JJ = 1 cm (⅜ in).

Draw new crotch.

P to PP = N to NN = 1 cm (⅜ in) for group 1,
1.5 cm (⅝ in) for group 2.

Draw inside leg JJ, Q, PP.

M to MM = 3 cm (1¼ in) for group 1,
2.5 cm (1 in) for group 2.

I to II = 1 cm (⅜ in) for group 1,
1.5 cm (⅝ in) for group 2.

Draw side seam MM, II, O, NN.

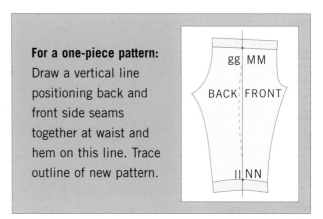

For a one-piece pattern: Draw a vertical line positioning back and front side seams together at waist and hem on this line. Trace outline of new pattern.

- Add 1 cm (⅜ in) seams all round.
- Add 4 cm (1⅝ in) to waist and hem for casings.

---

fabric suggestions

Tracksuits are usually cut in fleece, which can be plain, brushed or double-brushed as for polar fleece. Other fabrics such as Triacetate, brushed nylon (suitable for pyjamas), fancy knits and even some wovens are also acceptable tracksuit fabrics. Closely knitted fabric is less likely to bag at the knee, while nylon is usually lined with a thin cotton knit or towelling. Traditionally, sweat-shirts have ribbed necks, cuffs and hems, although some are just hemmed with side slits. Ribbing that contains Lycra will provide more stability to cuffs.

to sew

SWEATSHIRT

1 Select a suitable fleece fabric and matching rib, and interfacing if required.

2 Lay up the fabric and cut out the sweatshirt, following the grain lines very carefully. If applicable, fuse interfacings.

3 Follow steps 3 to 8 of the instructions given for the T-shirt on pages 32–33.

4 With right sides facing, match and pin the under-arm seams. Stitch one continuous seam from the hem of the sweatshirt to the hem of the sleeve. Trim the seam allowances to 6 mm (¼ in) when overlocking, then press.

5 For a ribbed cuff, establish the finished width of the cuff and cut twice the width plus 12 mm (½ in) for seams. Measure the length snugly around the wrist and add 12 mm (½ in) for seams. With right sides facing and raw edges together, fold in half widthwise and stitch the seam.

6 With wrong sides facing, fold the cuff in half lengthwise and divide into four equal parts. Mark with pins. Divide the sleeve hem into four equal parts and pin.

7 With right sides together, pin the cuff to the sleeve, matching the seams and aligning the pins. With the cuff side up, stitch the cuff to the sleeve, stretching the cuff to lie flat against the edge of the sleeve.

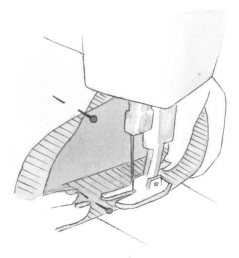

8 Overlock the edges and then press the seam towards the sleeve.

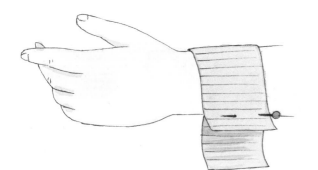

9 For an elasticated cuff, turn the casing towards the inside along the marked hemline and pin in position. Stitch, as illustrated, leaving a small opening through which to thread the elastic. Stitch another row close to the folded edge.

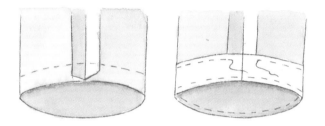

10 Measure elastic snugly around wrist and add 1–2 cm (⅜–¾ in) for the overlap. Cut and, using a bodkin or safety pin, thread the elastic through the casing. Be sure not to twist the elastic. Overlap the ends and stitch, as illustrated. Edgestitch the opening.

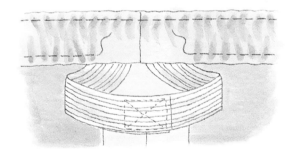

11 For the ribbing on the hem, repeat steps 5 to 8 (page 42). Measure the length of the ribbing around the upper hip.

12 For a plain hem, topstitch as required.

PANTS

1 Select the appropriate fabric (and ribbing, if required), lay it up and cut out strictly according to the grain lines.

2 Stitch front and back crotch seams and overlock the edges. Press. Join the side seams, aligning the notches and crotch seams. Stitch a continuous seam from the hem of one leg to the hem of the other. Overlock the edges and press. For lined pants, repeat this step, using the lining.

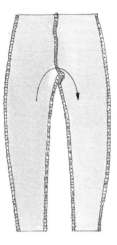

3 Overlock the waist and hem edges. For lined pants, overlock the lining together with the fabric at the waist and hem edges and continue as one piece of fabric.

4 For ribbed cuffs, follow steps 5 to 8 of the sweatshirt (page 42). Measure the length of the ribbing snugly around the ankle.

5 For elasticated waist and cuffs, follow steps 9 and 10 of the sweatshirt (see this page). Measure the elastic snugly around the waist and ankles.

6 For a straight hem, topstitch hem as desired.

embellishing

Creating a tracksuit for your child can be very rewarding. Here are some ideas to throw around as you decide what to do. Embroider flowers, stars or boats onto sweatshirts or track pants. Colour block by cutting sleeves and yokes in contrast colours. Appliqué numbers to the sleeves and chest. Stitch cargo pockets on the sides of pants, insert corded binding or add a contrast panel. Hoods with drawstrings keep away the chills: attach a collar and a short zip for a smarter look.

leggings

This fitted leg covering extends from the waist to the thigh, knee or ankle. Leggings have been worn since the Middle Ages as protection against the cold, and were fashionable children's wear from the 1850s until the early 1900s. In the 1980s they re-emerged as a fashion item and even today they are an essential garment in a child's wardrobe. They may be fitted at the ankle, fastened under the instep or flared into bell-bottoms. Essentially cut in a knitted fabric, preferably with a Lycra content to allow for extra stretch, leggings are easy to wear and look good with a printed sweatshirt or funky T-shirt. They can even be adapted into jodhpurs for horse-riding by using a firm, ribbed Lycra.

leggings pattern

Leggings have a snug fit and require stretch fabrics, preferably with a percentage of Lycra or elastic thread. Generally, the body measurements will denote the finished size of the pattern, but this will also depend on the amount of stretch in the fabric used. Use these instructions as a guide – it is easier to trim off the width of the leggings than to add more fabric when the garment is made up.

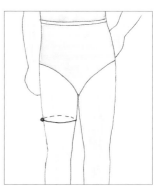

MEASUREMENTS REQUIRED

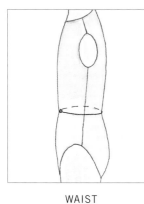
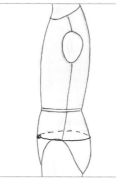
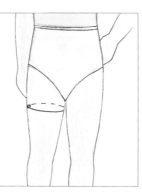

WAIST

HIP

UPPER THIGH

MID THIGH

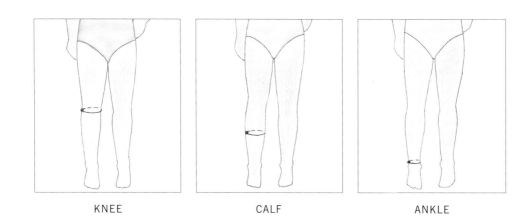

KNEE

CALF

ANKLE

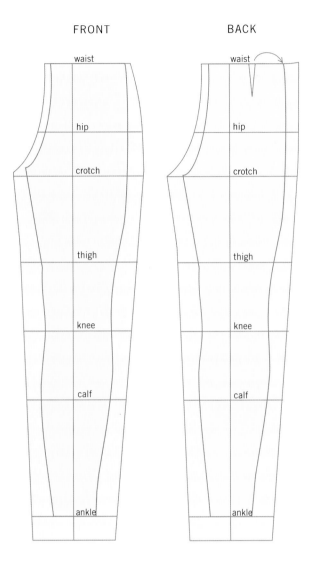

FRONT   BACK

waist

hip

crotch

thigh

knee

calf

ankle

- Add 6 mm (¼ in) seams for mock safety stitch.
- Position notches at strategic matching points.
- Add 1.5 cm (⅝ in) hem.
- Add 2–3 cm (¾–1¼ in) for elastic casing.
- Elastic is not above the waist as with other pants.
- For cycling shorts, crop above the knee.
- The pattern may be further reduced, depending on fabric used.

fabric suggestions

The most suitable fabrics to use are those that stretch but do not stretch out. Various cotton knits, polyester knits, nylon knits, ribbing and other fancy knits, all of which contain Lycra or a similar elastic thread, are found in this category. This allows the garment to recover its shape once it has been stretched out, for example, at the knee. Today, stretch woven fabrics with Lycra have been created, many of which, providing they are supple enough, will be suitable for leggings.

- Use a mock safety stitch, also known as 4-thread overlocking, for all seams.
- Alternatively, use a stretch stitch on your sewing machine and overlock the edges.
- Use bulk nylon floss thread, which allows more stretch to the stitch and prevents the seams from splitting under strain.
- Be sure to cut accurately according to the given grain lines. If not, the legs will twist and be uncomfortable to wear.

Trace outline of basic trouser block (page 24).
Reduce evenly, according to body measurements, at levels indicated.
Remove waist dart from side seam.
Shorten to ankle length.

to sew

1 Select a suitable stretch fabric, lay up and cut out the leggings following the grain lines very carefully.

2 Stitch the front and back crotch seams. Press.

3 Stitch the side seams, aligning the notches. Press.

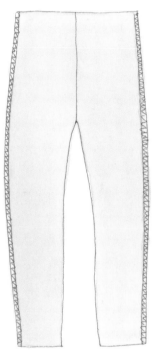

4 Join the inside leg seams, aligning the notches and crotch seams. Stitch continuously from the hem of one leg to the hem of the other leg.

5 Overlock the waist and hem edges.

Leggings fitted at the ankle and flared into bell-bottoms.

6 For the elasticated waist, follow steps 9 and 10 of the sweatshirt on page 43. Measure the elastic snugly around the waist.

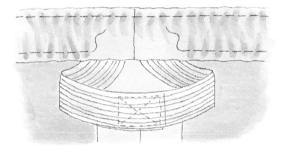

7 Topstitch hem and press garment.

embellishing

Leggings can be worn at any desired length. Above-the-knee cycling shorts are ideal for summer. Three-quarter or below-the-knee looks good with a small slit in the side seam. Ankle length may be fitted or flared, depending on the fashion of the day. Trim hems with frills, or add contrast piping to seams; small patch pockets come in handy for extra sweets. Prints, plains, stripes or ribbing, as long as it's knitted, will work for leggings.

trousers and shorts

Trousers have always been a popular garment for children. The basic block can easily be adapted into the current season's shape – baggy, fitted or bell-bottomed. They can even be cropped to make shorts. We all know how functional shorts are for children. Simple running shorts can be 'run' up in no time, and just think of the money saved! Denim jeans are not as daunting to make as they may seem, it's just a matter of shaping the pockets and back yoke and topstitching two rows in ochre or white along the relevant seams. Pockets or patches, loops or tabs, bows or buttons, embroidery or studs – there are endless ways of embellishing a simple trouser.

trouser pattern

The basic trouser block (page 24) can be adapted for all styles of trousers and shorts and it is unnecessary and time-consuming to reconstruct new patterns for each application. The basic block incorporates the ease required for a standard fit. The width and shape of the trouser is a matter of style and should be altered accordingly. The size and positioning of pockets and tucks will also depend on the design, but must be in proportion to the complete garment.

MEASUREMENTS REQUIRED

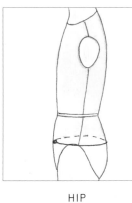

HIP

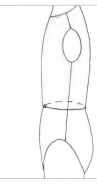

WAIST

CROTCH

INSIDE LEG

TROUSER WITH PLEATED FRONT AND ELASTIC BACK

These trousers are commonly used for school wear, but with the right choice of fabric and a bit of reshaping, they can easily be made into trendy Chinos.

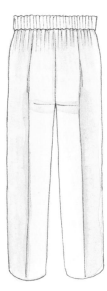

FRONT

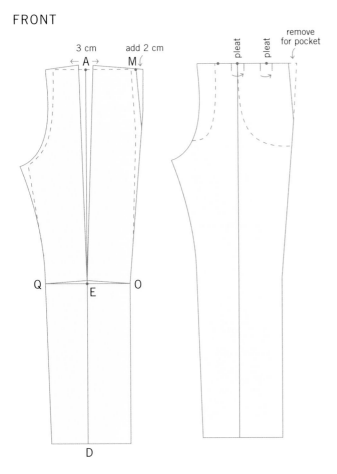

3 cm add 2 cm

A   M

Q   O

E

D

pleat pleat remove for pocket

STEP 1:

Trace outline of trouser front.

Mark in centre line AED.

Slash from A down to E and across to Q and O.

Spread A about 3 cm (1¼ in)

Add 2 cm (¾ in) at waist side seam to nothing at hip.

- When slashing to a specific point, be sure not to slash through that point, unless instructed to do so. Usually, the pattern pieces need to remain attached to maintain accuracy.

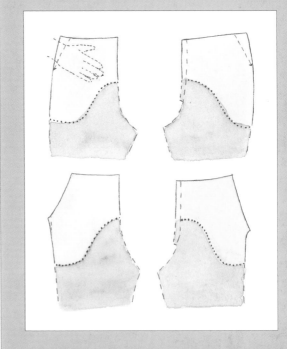

- Use the child's hand as a guide when establishing the pocket and opening size.
- The fly on boys' trousers laps left over right, but right over left for girls' trousers.
- Young children do not require a functional fly if the back is elasticated; a mock fly will suffice.

STEP 2:

Establish size of pocket opening and mark on pattern.

Mark 1st pleat at A.

Mark 2nd pleat halfway between A and pocket opening.

2nd pleat = 2 cm (¾ in).

STEP 3:

Establish size and shape of pocket bag.

Trace off pocket including wedge removed for opening.

Trace off pocket facing.

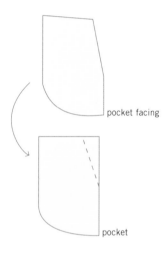

Trousers should be comfortable enough to wear when running and jumping around.

STEP 4:

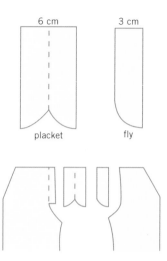

Establish the length of zip required for fly.

Trace off reverse copy of front.

Add 1 cm to right front crotch, from the waist to 1 cm (⅜ in) beyond the zip length.

Make placket as illustrated above, 6 cm (2⅜ in) wide to fit right crotch.

Make fly facing as illustrated above, 3 cm (1¼ in) wide for left front.

Reverse these details for girls' trousers, if required (see box below).

The difference between a girls' fly and a boys' fly is becoming less relevant today, and most girls wear the closing left over right, as do the boys.

For a mock fly:

Include fly onto front crotch, as illustrated.

BACK

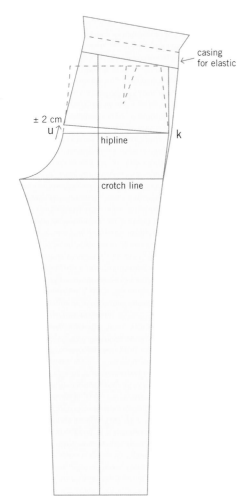

casing
for elastic

± 2 cm
u↑

hipline

k

crotch line

STEP 1:

Trace outline of back.

Mark u and k on hip.

Slash from u to k.

Spread about 2 cm (¾ in) at u.

Add 1.5 cm (⅝ in) to waist side seam to nothing at crotch line.

Erase dart.

Establish width of waist elastic.

Add double that width to back waist for casing (if required).

STEP 2:

Measure front waist of patterns.

To the right front include 1 cm (⅜ in) plus 3 cm (1¼ in) width from folded placket.

Make width to correspond with back casing.

Make right and left front waistband patterns accordingly.

(Right band must be 4 cm (1⅝ in) longer than left band.)

Make solid waistband as per illustration below.

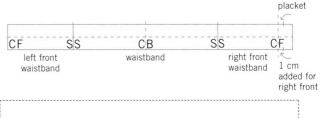

add 3 cm
for folded
placket

CF   S S   CB   S S   CF

left front
waistband

waistband

right front
waistband

1 cm
added for
right front

- Add 1 cm (⅜ in) seams to all pattern pieces.
- Add 3 cm (1¼ in) for hems.

Wear trousers and jeans full length, cropped or rolled up.

jeans pattern

Denim jeans are hard-wearing and very practical for children to wear. They may be baggy or slim-fitting. The back detail is probably more suitable for older children, whereas the elasticated back is more practical for younger children.

FRONT

STEP 1:
Trace outline of trouser front.
Establish size and shape of pocket opening.
Mark on pattern.

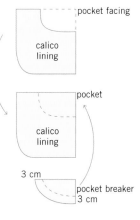

pocket facing

calico lining

pocket

calico lining

3 cm

pocket breaker
3 cm

STEP 2:
Establish size of pocket bag and mark.
Trace off pocket including shape removed for opening (breaker).
Trace off pocket facing.

When using a thick or heavy fabric for the trouser, a calico lining should be used for the pockets. If so, a pocket breaker needs to be made. Trace off the piece removed for the pocket opening, adding 3 cm (1¼ in) to the curved edge. This piece will then be stitched onto the calico pocket piece.

STEP 3:
Follow instructions for Pleated trousers step 4:
Fly, Placket and Fronts on page 56.

BACK

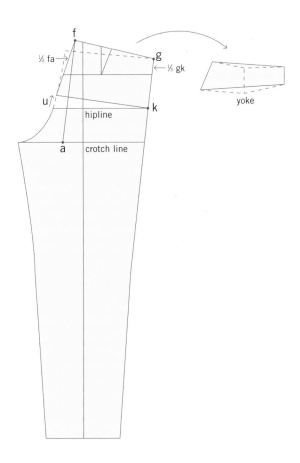

STEP 1:
Trace outline of back.

Mark u and k on hip.

Slash from u to k.

Spread about 2 cm (¾ in).

Mark yoke ⅓ fa at centre back and ⅓ gk at side seam.

Remove yoke and close dart.

Re-mark yoke and straighten lines, as illustrated.

> • Add 1 cm (⅜ in) seams to all pattern pieces.
> • Add 3 cm (1¼ in) for hems.

STEP 2:
Establish size and shape of back pocket.

Position on back, parallel to yoke seam.

STEP 3:
Follow instructions for Pleated trousers step 6: Waistband on page 58.

fabric suggestions

Various fabrics can be used for trousers and jeans, but denim, corduroy, tweed, cotton twill, canvas and other durable fabrics are most suitable for young children. Softer cottons can also be used for girls' wear. When using tartans or other large checks, determine whether the design is uneven or not before laying up the pattern, then align the panels to match one another. Align patterns so that the checks match along strategic or obvious seams (see below). Always cut corduroy in one direction only to avoid shading.

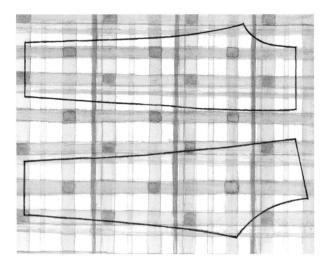

to sew

1 Select an appropriate fabric and compatible interfacing.

2 Lay up the fabric and cut out the trousers, following the grain lines and other patterns carefully. Cut the interfacings accordingly.

3 Fuse the interfacings on the waistband and pockets.

4 For the trouser, pin the front tucks in position and reinforce by stitching across the top just outside the seam line.

5 For the jeans, attach the back yokes and topstitch. Attach back pockets and topstitch down.

6 With right sides facing, pin and stitch the pocket facing to the garment along the opening edge of the pocket. Press flat, then trim seams, clipping or notching out the curves.

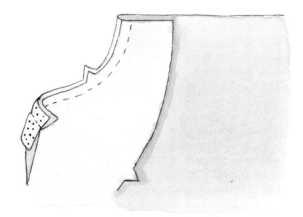

7 Press the seam open, and then press both towards the facing. Understitch the facing close to the seam line and through all the layers. Turn the facing towards the inside and press. Topstitch, if required.

8 For calico-lined pockets, overlock curved edge of pocket breaker. With right side facing, position on top of pocket and stitch down along the overlocked edge. Secure breaker to the pocket along waist and side edges.

9 With right sides together, pin and stitch the pocket to the facing. Press and overlock the edges. Secure the pocket to the front along the waist and side seam by stitching just outside the seam line.

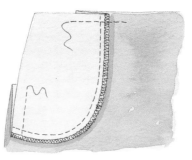

10 For the mock fly, stitch centre front seam with right sides together, stitching around fly and crotch. Overlock, press crotch and fly towards left or right front (see box on page 55 for fly positioning), and topstitch the fly through all the layers.

11 For an opening fly, stitch the fly facing to the left front, with right sides together. Overlock the edges of the facing, left front crotch and right front crotch.

12 Press the seam flat, so that the edges face the garment. Align the zip, facing down, with the seam line. Pin in place and, using a zip foot, stitch from the top downwards, on the facing side, close to the teeth.

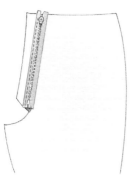

13 Stitch the bottom seam of the placket, then turn to the right side and press. Overlock the vertical edge of the placket.

14 First place the overlocked edge to the left-hand side and then position the other side of the zip, facing upwards, on top of the placket. Lastly, position the right front, right side down, on top of the zip. Ensure that all edges are aligned. Pin in place and stitch.

15 Turn over and stitch the crotch from the bottom at the inside leg to just beyond the seam line of the fly and then backstitch.

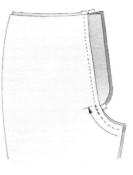

16 Turn the garment to the right side, fold the fly back on the seam line and press. Secure the fly with pins, keeping the placket aside to prevent it from being caught in the stitching. Mark the fly with tailor's chalk and topstitch. Reinforce the bottom of the fly, vertically, with a bartack.

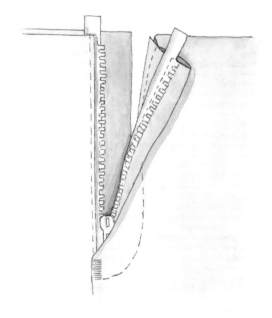

17 For the elasticated back, stitch the back crotch seam, overlock the edges, press and topstitch, if required. Overlock the back waist edge. Establish the elastic length required, usually about 7.5 cm (3 in) shorter than the pattern edge, and, with the elastic on the wrong side of the garment, stitch ends to the side seam allowances. Pin centre of the elastic to the centre of the back, fold over and topstitch casing.

- Elastic may be overlocked or zigzagged onto the back waist edge. This eliminates the overlocked edge as it is done in one operation.
- The mock fly front requires a one-piece front waistband. Attach as for the button front with the elasticated back.

18 With right sides facing, fold the front waistbands in half lengthwise and stitch across the centre front ends. Trim the corners, turn to the right side and press. Staystitch the waistline seam and, with right sides facing, attach the outside of the waistbands to the fronts, ensuring that the edges of the waistbands are flush with the edges of the fronts.

19 Pin the side seams together folding the front waistband over the back elasticated waistband at the side seams, as illustrated. Join the side seams, aligning the notches, overlock the edges, press and topstitch, if required. Topstitch the front waistbands down or 'stitch in the ditch'.

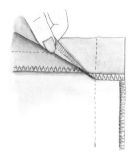

20 Join the inside leg seam, aligning the notches and the crotch seams, stitching continuously from the hem of the one leg to the hem of the other leg. Overlock the edges and press.

21 For the fitted waistband, first join the side seams, overlock the edges, press and topstitch, if required. Join the inside leg, as described above. Make belt loops, if required, attach to waistline and then attach the waistband as described in step 18. Topstitch the waistband down or 'stitch in the ditch'. Stitch belt loops down and bartack to secure.

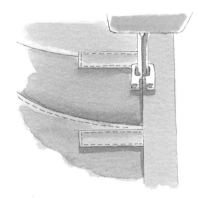

22 Hem the trousers by machine or by hand and stitch buttonhole and button in place.

shorts patterns

Shorts are easily adapted from the trouser pattern. Baggy pants can simply be cropped to the required length. Depending on the style, the leg circumference is usually increased, but for running shorts, it is decreased for a closer fit around the leg. Pedal pushers have a snug fit on the leg and some Capri pants are slightly flared at the hem.

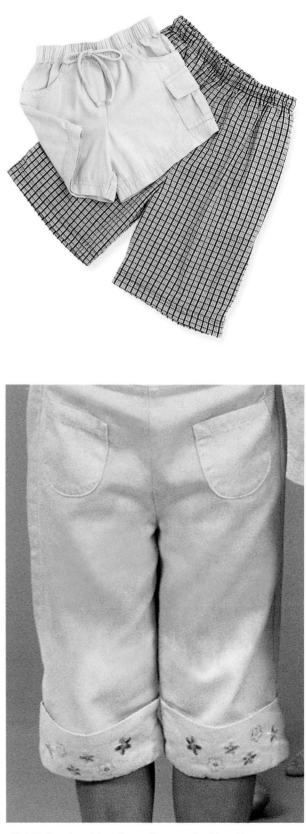

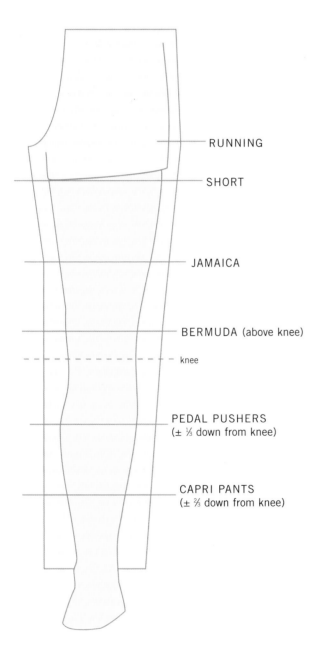

RUNNING

SHORT

JAMAICA

BERMUDA (above knee)

knee

PEDAL PUSHERS
(± ⅓ down from knee)

CAPRI PANTS
(± ⅔ down from knee)

Slightly flared pedal pushers with an embroidered hem.

ELASTICATED SHORTS

Establish length and width required.

Trace tracksuit pants back and front (pages 40–41), marking off at required length, squaring hem with the grainline.

Add to width by extending hem circumference, as desired.

For turn-ups, add double required depth to hem allowance.

Eliminate all waist darts.

Waist may be increased at side seam, if desired.

Reshape side seams accordingly.

Add casing at waist according to elastic width.

Add 1 cm (⅜ in) seams.

Add 3 cm (1¼ in) hems.

RUNNING SHORTS

Use tracksuit pants pattern (pages 40–41).

Mark inside leg about 4 cm (1⅝ in) down from crotch.

Curve hem up to crotch line at side seam, as illustrated.

Suppress hem 1–2 cm (⅜–¾ in) for a snug fit.

Adjust hem curve.

Add casing to waist.

Add 6 mm (¼ in) seams to crotch and side seams, tapering off to nothing at the hem.

No seams required at hem (usually bound).

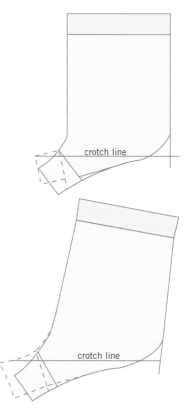

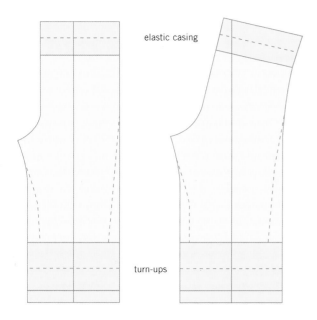

elastic casing

turn-ups

crotch line

crotch line

- Both wovens and knits are suitable, but your choice of fabric will depend on the style required.
- For sewing sequence, follow instructions given for tracksuit pants (page 43).

fabric suggestions

Knits and wovens are both suitable for these shorts. Cotton is more absorbent although synthetics dry quicker when wet. Establish for what purpose the shorts will be worn and select the fabric accordingly. Use a lightweight knit or soft fabric for the binding so that it feels comfortable against the skin.

to sew

1 Select the appropriate fabric, lay it up and cut out the shorts, following the grain lines carefully.

2 Join the backs to the fronts along the inside leg. Mark seam line on side seams.

3 With right sides facing, pin and stitch the binding from the waist, down the side seam of the back, along the hem edge and up the side seam of the front to the waist edge.

4 Fold the binding down and press seam. Wrap over seam allowances to the wrong side, encasing the seam allowance.

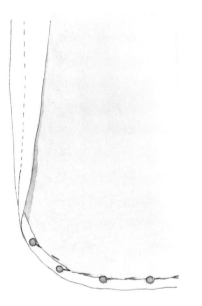

5 With right side up, 'stitch in the ditch' to secure the binding.

6 Lap bound front edge over back edge matching seam line marking. Pin in position and 'stitch in the ditch' from the waist to the start of the leg opening, stitching through all the layers.

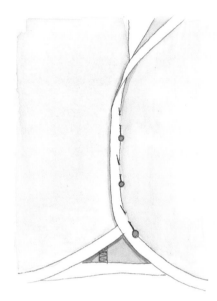

7 Slip one leg inside the other, with right sides together, and pin and stitch the crotch seam from the front to the back. Reinforce this seam with a double row of stitching.

8 Measure the elastic snugly around the waist and add 1–2 cm (⅜–¾ in) for the overlap.

9 Join the elastic and overlock it onto the wrong side of the waist edge, fold over towards the inside and topstitch down. Alternatively, encase the elastic as instructed for the sweatshirt in steps 9–10 on page 43.

It is advisable to use a mock safety stitch for the inside leg and crotch seams. Alternatively, use a stretch stitch and overlock the edges.

embellishing

Baggy shorts can be trimmed with pockets and contrast binding. Two rows of topstitching will add a finishing touch. Stitch a wrap onto the front of shorts for a faux skirt, and add frills at the hem of denim shorts to soften the look. Drawstring waists are great for girls; attach elastic between the ties for a better fit. Let your child paint designs on the trouser legs with fabric paints. Patches and appliqués can be stitched or ironed on.

dungarees

Dungarees were worn by workmen in the early 1900s and adopted for wear by women during the war. They soon became popular among children wanting to emulate their parents. As the denim dungaree became a fashion item in the 1950s for adults, so did it for children, and it has remained a winner ever since. With adaptable straps, pockets and flaps they prove to be most useful for playtime. Dungarees can be worn with thin T-shirts or thick pullovers, dolled up with frills or lace for the girls, or made to resemble work overalls for the boys. Use your creative skills to design your own style, or ask your children for their input. Whatever you decide, dungarees are a must for all kids!

dungarees pattern

Dungarees are very practical, especially for younger children. They are usually loose-fitting and therefore comfortable to wear. They can consist of pants and a bib with straps or pants extended up to a yoke with straps. Dungarees are usually worn over T-shirts, shirts or even jerseys.

- For gathers, lightweight fabrics will require more fullness than will, for example, corduroy.
- Fold tucks on paper to determine the shaping at the seam.
- Width of facings may be from 3–5 cm (1¼–2 in).
- Straps can be cut longer than required to allow for growth of child.

MEASUREMENTS REQUIRED

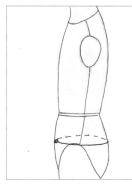

HIP

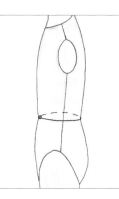

WAIST

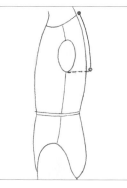

ARMHOLE DEPTH

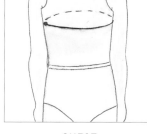

CHEST

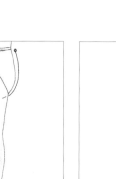

CROTCH

INSIDE LEG

FRONT

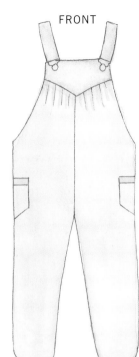

BACK

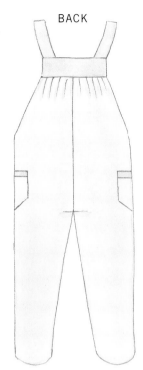

FRONT

STEP 1:
Align basic trouser front (page 24) with front bodice (page 16), meeting at waist. Ensure that centre front crotch and bodice form a straight line. Mark yoke and armhole shaping, as desired. Measure distance from yoke to shoulder.

STEP 2:
Cut off yoke piece. Slash grain line down to E and across to Q and O. Spread to allow for gathers or tucks (see box on page 70). Mark armhole facing. Trace yoke with centre on fold, as illustrated. Establish shape, size and positioning of pocket.

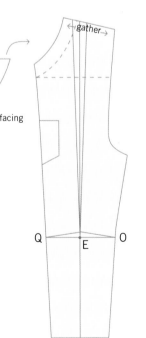

BACK

STEP 1:

Align basic trouser back
(page 24) with bodice
back (page 16).
Zg = ZM on front.
Mark yoke and armhole
shaping to balance
with front.
Straighten centre
back line from bottom
of yoke to hipline.
Measure distance from
yoke to shoulder.

STEP 2:

Slash hipline from centre
back to side seam.
Raise about 3 cm (1¼ in)
to lengthen crotch.

- Add 1 cm (⅜ in) seams all round.
- Add 3 cm (1¼ in) for hems.
- Cut yokes double.

STEP 3:

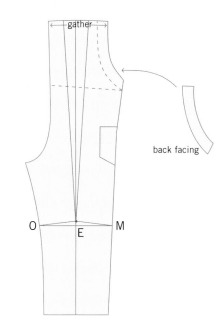

Cut off yoke piece.
Slash grain line down to E and
across to O and M.
Spread to allow for gathers or tucks.
Mark armhole facing.
Trace yoke with centre on fold.
Mark pocket position.

STEP 4:

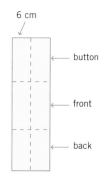

Make strap 3 cm (1¼ in) wide on fold.
Determine length from measurements
taken on front and back.
Add to length of strap for button, allowing
a little extra for growth.

fabric suggestions

Durable fabrics such as denim, corduroy, tweed, canvas and cotton twill are the popular fabrics from which to choose. Today, however, fleece, knits and other lightweight prints have been used very successfully. This will depend entirely on the styling of the dungarees. Lightweight fabrics will require interfacing on the straps and yokes for stability and to secure the buttonholes. All pocket facings or hems should be interfaced.

to sew

1 Select the appropriate fabric, lay it up and cut out the dungarees, following the grain lines closely. Cut and fuse the necessary interfacings and press back the pocket seams.

2 Join the side seams, aligning the notches, then overlock the edges and press the seams flat. Hem the pockets, position them over the side seams, as desired, and stitch down. Reinforce the top corners as illustrated below.

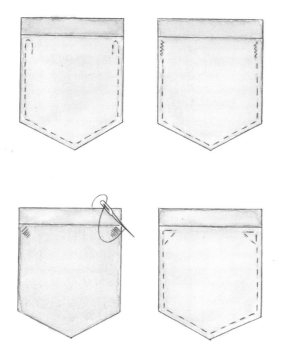

3 Stitch the back and front crotch seams and overlock the edges. Press. Join the inside leg seam, aligning the notches and the crotch seams, stitching continuously from the hem of one leg to the hem of the other leg. Overlock the edges and press.

4 With right sides facing, stitch around the edge of the straps, leaving one short end open for turning. Trim off the excess seam allowances at the corners and turn to the right side. Press flat and topstitch, if required.

5 Gather the back and front evenly to fit their corresponding yokes and attach to these yokes. Pin the straps in position on the back yoke and stitch down securely. (Follow gathering instructions for the dress with yoke, steps 6 and 7, on page 102.)

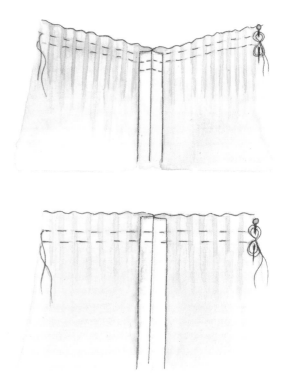

6 Attach the armhole facings to the matching yoke facings and at the side seams. Overlock the outside edges. Pin the complete facing onto the garment, matching the notches, and stitch down. Trim the seam allowances and press towards the facing. Stitch on the right side of the facing, close to the seam line.

Understitching is used to keep the facings from rolling to the right side of the garment. Stitch as close to corners as your machine will allow.

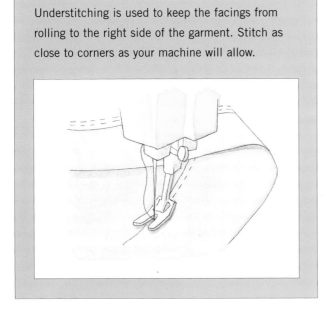

7 Topstitch around the yokes to match the straps. Stitch buttonholes on the front yoke and attach buttons to fit the straps. Stitch hem and press.

8 For an elasticated waist, attach casing along marked waistline. Establish elastic measurement required, allowing 1–2 cm (⅜–¾ in) for the overlap and thread the elastic through the casing using a bodkin. Overlap the ends and stitch. Stitch the opening closed.

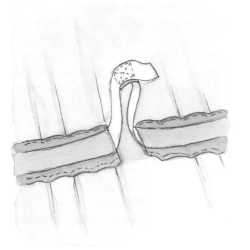

Traditional denim dungarees with topstitching.

embellishing

Canvas and denim dungarees are usually trimmed with lots of contrast topstitching in either one or two rows. It is easier to topstitch after each seam has been sewn rather than when the garment is completed. Pockets with various compartments, mock flies and metal buttons create a work-wear look. Trim with labels, patches or appliqués. Elasticate baggy waists for a better fit. Use the dungaree details to create a pinafore for girls.

anoraks

The anorak was originally worn by Eskimos and was made of seal-skin. Today this windbreaker is usually made of nylon waterproof or water-repellent fabric. This garment can be lined according to specific requirements: for a basic anorak, use towelling or cotton knit; for a warmer jacket, use fun fur to line the body and towelling for the sleeves. For extra insulation, you can even quilt the fabric with a man-made fibre-fill or wadding. The hood, sleeves and hem can be trimmed with fake fur for an alpine look. The adventurous seamstress may even attempt stitching a hood that zips away into a collar. All children need protection from the wind and rain and will find the anorak very comfortable and useful.

anorak pattern

All children need an anorak for wet weather. They are quite simple to make and should rather be oversized than too small. The sweatshirt pattern (pages 39–40) can be adapted for this use. The extension to the pattern can be varied, but the proportions should remain the same.

MEASUREMENTS REQUIRED FOR THE HOOD

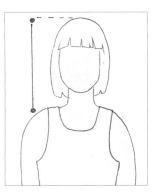

HEAD TO SHOULDER

FOREHEAD TO NAPE

Anorak with tab detail fastening the hood.

FRONT AND BACK

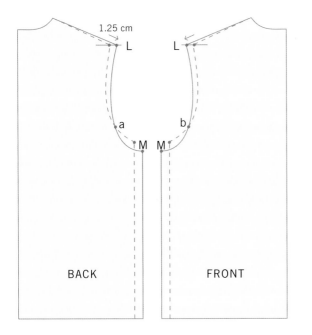

SLEEVE

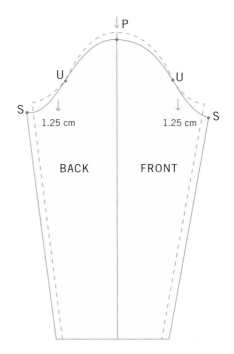

Trace outline of back and front sweatshirt pattern (page 39).

Extend shoulder by 1.25 cm (½ in).

Drop armhole by 2.5 cm (1 in).

Extend armhole by 2 cm (¾ in).

Extend back and front body length, as desired.

Mark a and b as illustrated.

Trace outline of sweatshirt sleeve (page 40).

Mark U, and U, and P on crown.

Drop P by 1.25 cm (½ in).

Drop underarm by 1.25 cm (½ in) (½ measurement armhole is dropped).

Extend underarm so that US = aM on the back and US = bM on the front.

Extend wrist by 1 cm (⅜ in) on either side.

RAGLAN CONVERSION

BACK AND FRONT

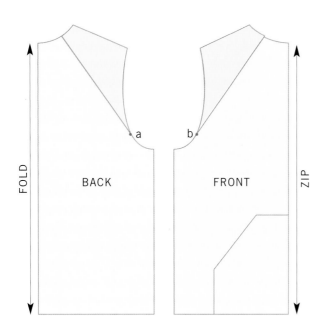

Mark raglan conversion as for T-shirt on page 30.
Establish size and position of pocket.

SLEEVE

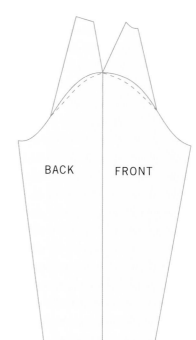

Position raglan panels on sleeve crown, as illustrated.
Sleeve may be split down centre grain line, if desired.

- Add 1.5 cm (⅝ in) seams to centre front for zip.
- Add 2.5 cm (1 in) to pocket opening and to hood edge for cord.
- Add 1 cm (⅜ in) seams all round.
- Add 3 cm (1¼ in) casings to sleeve and body hem, for elastic.
- For ribbed cuff, remove ½ cuff width from the hem of the sleeve.

Studded placket concealing the zip of this anorak.

HOOD

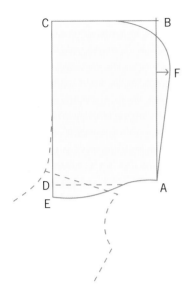

Mark back and front, matching shoulder seams.
AB = Shoulder to head.
Mark along centre back.
BC = AD = ½ back and front neck on pattern.
Square across.
BF = ¼ AB.
Extend by about 2 cm (¾ in).
Join A to F and curve to C, as illustrated.
DE = about 3 cm (1¼ in).
Draw curved line from E to back neck at shoulder.

STEP 6:
Make pocket pattern according to shape and size selected.
Mark pocket on front.

fabric suggestions

The anorak is worn for warmth and protection from wind and rain. Use a fabric that is made from a durable fibre such as nylon, or that gets its strength from a fine, tight weave. Waterproof fabrics are coated or laminated to prevent moisture from penetrating the fabric, but they are not porous and can make you perspire. Water-repellent fabrics will prevent a certain amount of water from penetrating the fabric, but prolonged exposure will eventually allow some water through. These fabrics are comfortable to wear and offer sufficient protection from the elements. Water-repellent, crinkled nylon is crease resistant and is the most suitable fabric for children's wear.

Lining the anorak is preferable but not essential, depending on its use. Knitted or woven towelling, cotton knit, brushed fleece and other woolly fabrics will provide warmth, but insulation will add extra warmth in very cold conditions. Use a polyester fibre-fill, available in various densities, to interline or quilt the lining.

- When cutting the lining, ascertain whether or not it stretches and, if so, by how much.
- Use the anorak pattern for the lining and interlining and trim off the excess in the length of the sleeves and body. This will vary depending on the fabrics used.
- If using interfacing, bear in mind that waterproof and most water-repellent fabrics cannot be ironed. A sew-in quality would have to be used.
- Run your nail along the seams to flatten them instead of pressing with an iron.

to sew

1 Select a suitable fabric and lining, if required.

2 Lay up the fabrics and cut out the anorak following the grain lines carefully.

3 Hem the pockets, turn under the seam allowances, pin in position and attach to the fronts.

4 Stitch the dart at the top of the sleeve (for one-piece) or join the overarm seam (for two-piece). Overlock the edges.

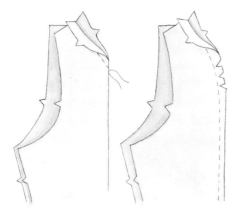

5 With right sides facing, pin and stitch the sleeve to the back and fronts, matching notches. Overlock the edges. If topstitching is required, fold seam allowance towards the garment and topstitch down.

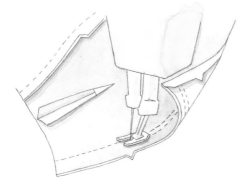

6 With right sides facing, pin and match the under-arm seams. Stitch from the hem of the garment to the hem of the sleeve. Overlock the edges.

7 Mark the buttonhole for the drawstring on the hood. Reinforce with a patch of interfacing, pinned in position. With right sides facing, pin and stitch the centre back seam of the hood. Overlock the edges.

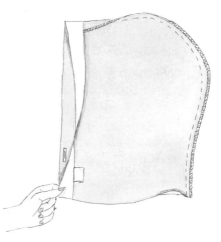

8 Overlock the centre front edges. Pin the one side of the zip in position along the centre front. For an elasticised hem, align the open end of the zip with the hemline. Using a zip foot, stitch the one side of the zip down and carefully align the other side so that the pocket seams match.

9 Fold the casing around the zip and stitch along the upper edge of the casing, as illustrated. Measure elastic to fit the hip generously and insert into casing. Stitch down across casing and elastic. Topstitch the zip from neck to hem, stitching through the elastic at the hem. Secure the ends with bartacks.

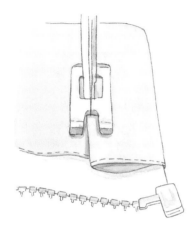

10 For a drawstring hem, align the open end of the zip about 1 cm (⅜ in) above the hemline to allow the drawstring to be threaded through. Stitch down one side of the zip; align the other side carefully, and stitch in place. Fold casing around the zip and on the hemline, leaving a gap for the drawstring. Topstitch the zip from the neck to the end of the zip, but not through the hem. Bartack in line with the end of the zip.

11 With right sides facing, pin the hood to the neck, aligning the notches carefully. Wrap the hem of the hood around the top of the zip and stitch. Overlock the edges. Topstitch the hem of the hood.

12 Overlock the sleeve hem edges. For a lined anorak, overlock the lining together with the fabric and continue as one piece of fabric. Fold the fabric towards the inside along the marked hemlines and stitch the casings, leaving a small opening to thread the elastic through. Measure the elastic snugly around the wrists, allowing 1–2 cm (⅜–¾ in) for the overlap. Cut and, using a bodkin or safety pin, thread the elastic through. Overlap ends and stitch elastic. Stitch opening closed.

13 For a lined anorak, follow the same sequence as the anorak. Attach the sleeves to the body and join hood. Attach lining hood and fabric hood to respective bodies. With right sides facing, sandwich the zip between the fabric and the lining and stitch. Join hood at hem. Push the hood between body and lining, as illustrated, aligning seams. Pin and stitch seam allowances together. Turn to the right side and overlock the lining and fabric together at the sleeve and body hems. Stitch casings, thread elastic and topstitch zip.

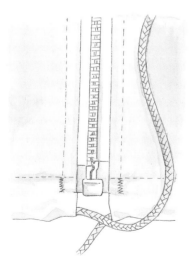

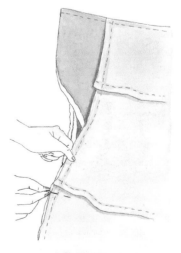

embellishing

Use buttons, poppers or a zip to affix a detachable hood to the collar of an anorak. Line the hood with a contrast print. Pockets are essential and can be positioned in the side seam or patched onto the anorak, preferably at hip level. Use hook and loop tape, buttons or poppers to fasten pocket flaps. Attach patches, embroideries or appliqués for decoration. For a snug fit add a drawstring to the waist or to the hem. Make sure that the anorak fit is generous.

skirts

Skirts are as popular today as ever before. They are worn at school, for sport and for smart wear. Whether pleated, gathered or flared, they can easily be trimmed into the trendiest styles. Tiered skirts can be edged with lace for a peasant look, while tartans can be pleated into kilts and petticoats can be added to lift flared skirts.

Denim skirts can be styled on the jeans' cut. Rickrack, braid, fringes or frills can enhance the plainest skirt. Wrap skirts work well for ballet or the beach. Appliqué a fun motif near the hem, or personalise the skirt with embroidered initials on the pocket. Add a bib and straps to create a pinafore. Hipster, high waist, maxi or mini, your daughter is bound to wear a skirt at some stage.

skirt patterns

The basic skirt block (pages 20–21) can be used to construct various styles. Waistbands may be fitted or elasticated depending on the design of the garment and age of the child. Gathered or pleated frills can be added to the hems, following the same method as for the skirt. The backs should preferably follow the same shape as the fronts; some skirts, however, are only pleated in front and have plain or elasticated backs.

MEASUREMENTS REQUIRED

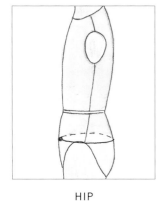

HIP

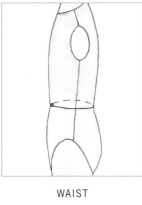

WAIST

Trace outline of skirt front.
Mark working line perpendicular to centre front.
Divide the waist into four equal parts, as illustrated.
For darted front, align these parts with darts,
as illustrated.

WITHOUT DARTS

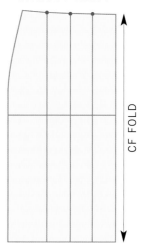

CF FOLD

WITH DARTS

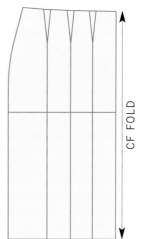

CF FOLD

FLARED SKIRT

GATHERED SKIRT

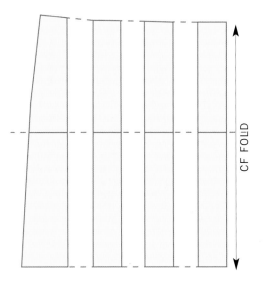

Cut along lines from hem through waist.
Draw second working line.
Spread panels according to the fullness required,
aligning the working lines.
Ignore any darts.
Repeat for backs.

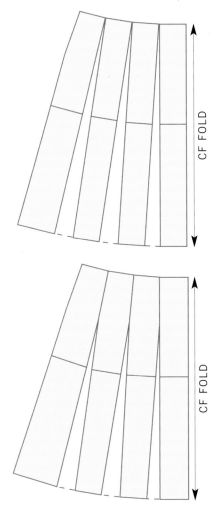

Cut along lines from hem to, but not through, waist.
Close darts where necessary and spread panels
evenly, as required.
Repeat for backs.

PLEATED SKIRT

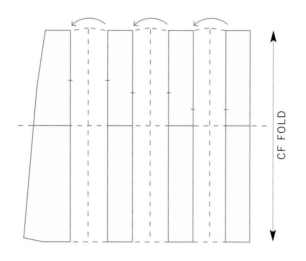

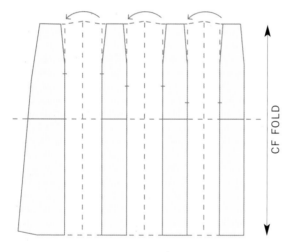

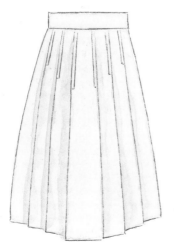

Follow instructions for gathered skirt (page 91).
Spread panels according to depth of pleat required, aligning working lines.
Incorporate darts into panels, as illustrated.
Notch pleat depth clearly.
Indicate stitchline of pleat.

Make waistband pattern to fit waist of basic skirt pattern (step 6, page 57).
Add 2.5 cm (I in) to length for button.
Establish width required.

For elasticated back:
Extend gathered back pattern at waist to include casing for elastic.
Ensure that front waistband is the same width as back elastic casing.

- Add 1.5 cm (⅝ in) seam to centre back for zip.
- Cut centre front on fold.
- Add 1 cm (⅜ in) seams all round.
- Add 3 cm (1¼ in) for hem.

Knife pleats are best made by professional pleaters.

fabric suggestions

Most fabrics are suitable for skirts. Firmly woven fabrics, such as denim, corduroy and canvas are most durable. Knits, such as interlock, jersey, fleece and cotton, are a good choice as they allow movement for active children. Gingham, madras cotton, seersucker, twill, voile, chambray and calico are also suitable. Natural fibres are non-abrasive, but synthetics are crease resistant. Choose a fabric that complements the design of the skirt.

to sew

1 Select an appropriate fabric and test interfacing for the waistband.

2 Lay up the fabric and cut out the skirt, following the grain lines carefully and pattern matching, where necessary. Fuse the waistband and press along the fold line.

3 Stitch darts, tucks, pleats or gathers at the waist and draw up where necessary. Skirts that require permanent pleating, should be hemmed at this stage.

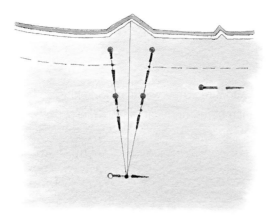

4 Overlock the edges of the seam requiring a zip and stitch, leaving an opening for the zip. Fold the seam allowances under and press.

5 With the right side of the garment facing up and the zip open, place the zip face down on the skirt with the teeth on the pressed seam line. Pin in position and stitch from the bottom to the top. Close the zip and fold back the seam allowance.

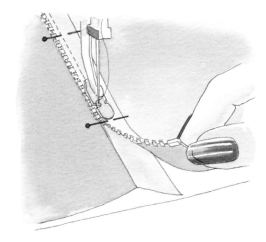

6 Position the pressed seam allowance on the free side of the zip so that the fold overlaps the teeth. Pin or glue in place and stitch across the bottom and up the side, pivoting at the corner and using a guide for the topstitching. Pull the threads through to the wrong side and secure.

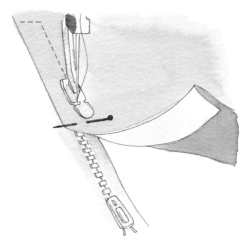

7 Attach any pockets at this stage. Stitch the side seams and any other seams, aligning the notches. Overlock the edges and press the seams.

8 Overlock the inside edge of the waistband. Fold in half lengthwise, with right sides facing, and stitch across both ends. Trim the seam allowances, turn to the right side and push out the corners. Press.

9 Staystitch the skirt waist seam line. With right sides together, pin the waistband to the skirt, carefully matching all the notches. Ensure that the left back edge of the waistband is flush with the edge of the zip, and that the underlap is on the right back side.

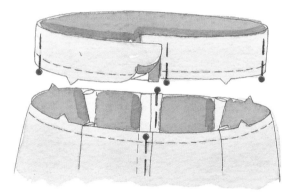

10 Stitch, easing the skirt if necessary, but be sure not to allow any tucks to form. Press, trim and clip the seam.

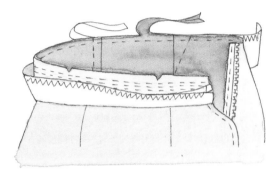

11 Turn to the right side and press the seam up towards the waistband. Fold up the seam allowance of the underlap and pin in place. With right side up, edgestitch the lower edge of the waistband, catching the overlocked seam of the waistband.

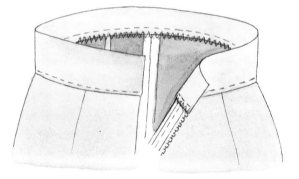

12 Stitch the hem, stitch the buttonhole on the waistband and attach the button.

embellishing

The skirt silhouette can vary from straight to flared or pleated. Hemlines need not necessarily be straight but may be pointed. Trim a V-hemline with sequins or beads; trim the waist with rhinestones or a belt; trim seams with lace edging or embroidered braid.

Use striped elastic or plait rope for a belt, or simply paint a design on a fabric belt. Combine prints with plain fabrics for an interesting feature. Use off-cuts from a blouse for a mix-and-match look. The sky's the limit!

dresses

Little girls always look cute in frilly dresses. Add a lace collar, pin tucks and pearly buttons for a Victorian style, or use contrast lining for lace fabric to create a different effect. Balance the use of lace, frills, bows and smocking to create a pretty party dress. Broderie anglaise or flocked voile dresses are sure winners, and a sundress with straps will be cool in summer. The pinafore, worn with tights and a pullover, is a winter favourite. Raise the waist for an empire line or drop the waist to the hip. Shirtwaist styles work for all ages, irrespective of the waist position. You can also panel the dress for more shape and flare. There are many suitable fabrics for dresses, but muslin is the most popular for summer, and corduroy for winter.

dress patterns

Dresses are easy to wear – just one item of clothing to slip on. Older girls might prefer to wear separates, depending on fashion trends, but little girls will always wear the dress with yoke. Younger girls usually wear high yokes and as they grow older the yoke moves closer to the waistline. The yoke may be as narrow as a facing or as wide as a dropped waist, but the method of construction remains the same. Use the basic dress block on pages 22–23 to create these classic dresses.

MEASUREMENTS REQUIRED

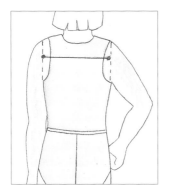

ACROSS BACK

NECK

CHEST

SINGLE SHOULDER

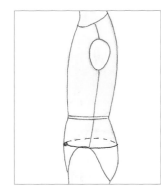

HIP

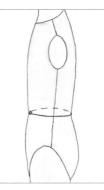

WAIST

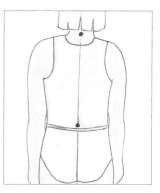

ARMHOLE DEPTH

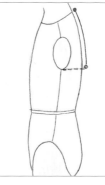

NAPE TO WAIST

DRESS WITH YOKE

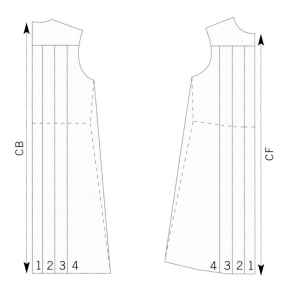

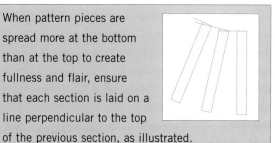

- When pattern pieces are spread more at the bottom than at the top to create fullness and flair, ensure that each section is laid on a line perpendicular to the top of the previous section, as illustrated.
- Heavier fabrics require less fullness and lightweight, soft fabrics require more. The average amount is double the finished width (i.e. 2:1).

Trace outline of dress back and front.

Establish width of yoke and mark on back and front.

Straighten side seam from underarm to hem.

Divide dress below yoke into four sections.

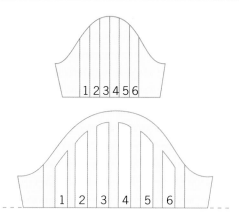

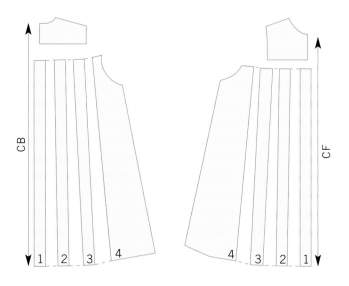

Cut out yokes and through sections.

Spread sections to desired width.

Establish sleeve length, including depth of frill, and trace outline of sleeve.

Divide sleeve into six sections, as illustrated.

Draw a line. Cut and spread sections to desired width along this line.

Add about 2 cm (¾ in) to sleeve head, as illustrated.

- Cut yoke and dress fronts on fold.
- Add 1.5 cm (⅝ in) seams to centre back for zip.
- Add 1 cm (⅜ in) seams all round.
- Yokes are self-faced. Cut double.
- For single yokes, cut neck facing to finish 4–5 cm (1⅝–2 in).
- Add 3 cm (1¼ in) for hem.
- Add 1 cm (⅜ in) for sleeve hem.
- For bound neck, do not add seams.

to sew

1 Select a suitable fabric, and lining and interfacing, if required.

2 Lay up the fabric and cut out the dress following the grain lines carefully. Fuse any interfacings.

3 Join the shoulder seams and overlock the edges. Join any facings. Press seams.

4 With right sides facing, pin and stitch together the necklines of the double yokes or yokes and facing combination. Trim the seam allowances to 6 mm (¼ in), turn to the right side and understitch close to the seam. Press. For a bound neck, attach the binding to neckline.

5 Double turn a narrow sleeve hem and stitch. Press. Cut 6 mm (¼ in) elastic to fit the arm comfortably, but not snugly, plus 1 cm (⅜ in) seam allowances. Mark the stitching line for the elastic on the wrong side of the sleeve using chalk or a washable marker. Pin the elastic to the wrong side of the sleeve along this line at the seams and midpoint. With the elastic facing up, zigzag it to the sleeve over this marked line, stretching to fit between the pins.

6 Lengthen the stitch setting and loosen the upper tension on the machine for gathering. With right side up, stitch two rows just to the outside of the stitch-line of the front and backs. With right sides facing, pin the front and backs to their corresponding yokes, aligning any notches. Draw up the bobbin threads so that the bodies fit into the yokes. Secure threads by twisting a figure eight around the pins. Adjust gathers uniformly and pin down perpendicular to the stitching.

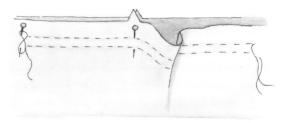

7 While the machine is set for gathering, gather the sleeve head between the notches as instructed in step 6. Reset the stitch length and tension on the machine. With gathered side up, attach the bodies to the yokes, stitching on the seam line, as illustrated. Hold the fabric on either side to avoid stitching little pleats. Overlock the seam and press the seam allowance up. Press the gathers, sliding the point of the iron up into them. Do not press across the gathers, as they will flatten and become limp.

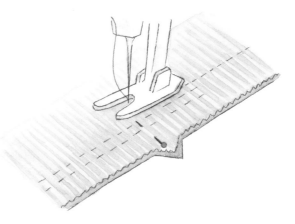

8 Draw up the gathers on the sleeve head and attach to the armhole following the instructions in steps 6 and 7 (page 102).

9 Overlock the centre back edges and stitch the seam, leaving the opening for the zip. Fold the seam allowances under and press. Place the zip face down just below the neckline and with the stopper just below the opening at the bottom. This will compel you to stitch across the zip above the stopper, securing the end and preventing needle breakage. Pin in position.

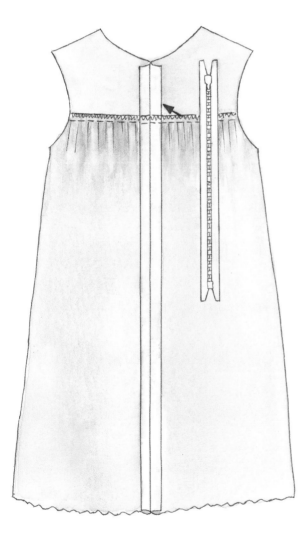

10 With the right side up and zip closed, and using a zip foot, stitch across the bottom of the zip and up the one side. Open the zip slightly to stitch past the slider. Leaving the needle down, lift the foot, move the slider past the needle and continue stitching. Move the zip foot to the other side, stitch across the bottom and up the other side of the zip in the same way. Ensure that the folded edge covers the teeth at all times. Pull threads through to the wrong side and secure.

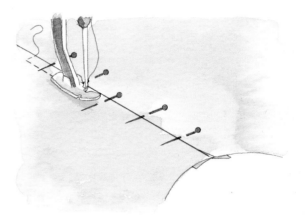

11 With right sides facing, pin the side seams together, aligning all seams and notches, and stitch from the hem of the sleeves to the hem of the dress. Overlock the edges and press. Bartack the seam allowance at the sleeve edge.

12 Pin the yoke lining down and slipstitch the lining to the armhole, yoke edge and centre back at the zip, encasing the seam allowances. Hem the dress and press.

> For a quicker application, stitch the yokes and their linings as one piece of fabric when attaching the sleeves and bodies, overlocking all the edges together.

DROPPED WAIST

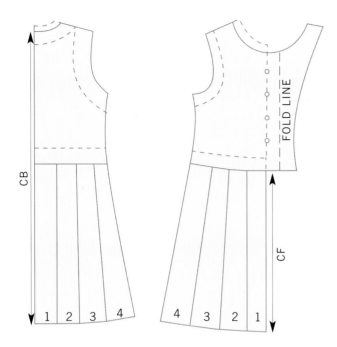

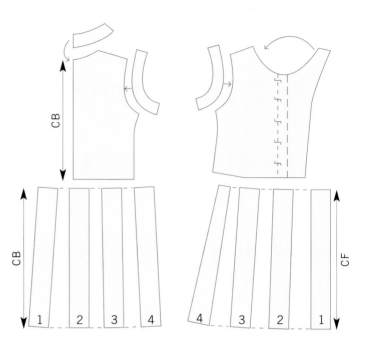

Trace outline of back and front dress.

Lower neckline by the required amount.

Establish position of waistline and mark it on the back and front.

Divide skirt into four sections.

Add 1.5 cm (⅝ in) to centre front; fold back on this line to trace off facing.

Cut out bodices and through sections.

Mark and cut out armhole facings and back neck facing.

Spread skirt sections as required.

- Cut centre back bodice and back and front skirt on fold.
- Add 1 cm (⅜ in) seams all round.
- Add 3 cm (1¼ in) for hems.
- Skirt may be gathered or pleated, as desired.
- If sleeves are required, eliminate sleeve facings.
- For bound armholes, do not add seam allowance.

to sew

1 Follow steps 1 to 4 for dress with yoke on page 102, joining the armhole facings at the shoulders and the back neck facing to the front facing, also at the shoulders. Overlock the outer edges of the facings.

2 With right sides facing, pin and stitch the armhole facing to the armhole, aligning the notches. Pin and stitch the back and front necks to the facings, matching the shoulder seams. Trim the seam allowances and understitch close to the edge. Press.

3 Gather the back and front skirts as instructed in steps 6 and 7 for dress with yoke on page 102. Be sure to overlap the bodice fronts, right over left, so that they meet at the centre front.

4 With right sides facing and seams aligned, stitch the side seams from the edge of the armhole facing to the hem. Overlock the edges and tack the facings down at the underarm and shoulders.

5 Mark buttonholes horizontally to extend the centre front line by 3 mm (⅛ in), as illustrated. Stitch buttonholes and attach buttons on the centre front line to correspond with the buttonholes.

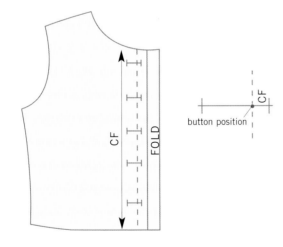

6 Stitch the hem and press.

fabric suggestions

Dresses with gathers require soft, lightweight fabrics such as voile, batiste, cotton knit, gingham, seersucker, flannel, chambray and muslin. Line lightweight fabrics with self-fabric or soft lining and transparent fabric with solid colour fabrics. Use narrow French seams on sheer fabric or overlock close to the stitchline. Heavyweight fabrics need not necessarily be stiff. Soft corduroy, denim and tweed are suitable for winter dresses and pinafores. Most knits, from interlock to fleece, will also work well for dresses.

Denim pinafore styled on the traditional dungaree.

PINAFORE

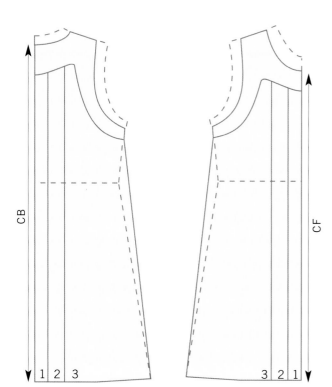

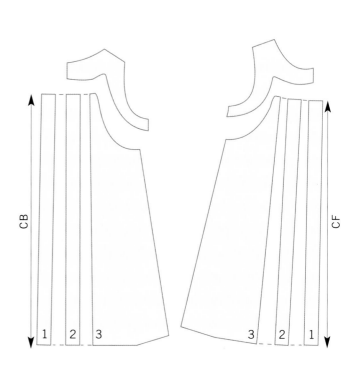

Trace outline of dress back and front.

Drop armholes approximately 1 cm (⅜ in) and neckline as required.

Straighten side seams from armhole to hem.

Mark curved yoke and divide remaining sections into three as illustrated above.

Cut out yokes and cut through panels.

Spread these sections to the required width.

- Cut centre front yoke and dress on the fold.
- Add 1.5 cm (⅝ in) seams to centre back yoke and dress for the zip.
- Add 1 cm (⅜ in) seams all round.
- Add 3 cm (1¼ in) for hems.
- Yokes are self-faced. Cut double.

to sew

1 Follow steps 1 and 2 for the dress with yoke on page 102; then continue with steps 6 and 7 on page 102 ignoring any reference to sleeves; and then follow steps 9 and 10 on page 103.

2 Join the front and back facings at the underarms and overlock the edges. With right sides facing, pin and stitch the back and front panels at the side seams, aligning the notches.

3 Pin a narrow tuck in the front and back shoulders of the dress: when released this will ensure that the facing seams do not show.

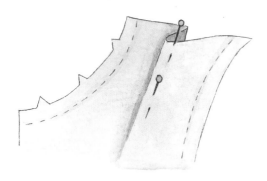

4 Pin the facing to the dress around the armholes and the front and back neckline. (NB The shoulder seams of the dress and the facings have not yet been joined.) Start stitching about 1 cm (⅜ in) away from the shoulder edges. Trim and clip the seam allowances.

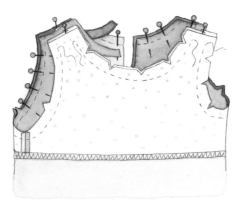

5 With the wrong side up, lightly press the seam allowances towards the facing. Turn the facing towards the inside and, with the facing side up, under-stitch close to the seam line where possible. Press.

6 Release the shoulder tucks. With the neck and the armhole seam allowances folded back and the facing folded out of the way, stitch the shoulder seams of the dress. Press the seams, first flat and then open, and push through the opening.

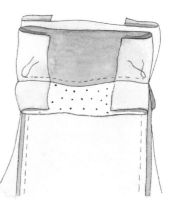

7 Trim the facing seam allowances, turn under and slipstitch by hand. Turn back the seam allowance of the facing at the centre back and press. Slipstitch in position and tack facings down at all strategic seams. Alternatively, 'stitch in the ditch' along the yoke seams.

8 Stitch the hem and press.

embellishing

Trims can make such a difference to a plain dress. Hand or machine embroidery always looks special; position it strategically on a yoke, bodice or pocket, or embroider along the entire hemline! Bows are feminine and can be used to add a finishing touch to a garment. Pockets, mock pockets or pocket flaps also add another dimension. Strap dresses are ideal for the summertime, and straps vary from wide bands to thin, shoestring ties. From prints to plains, the fabric choice is endless.

glossary

ABBREVIATIONS:
CF: Centre front
CB: Centre back
SS: Side seam

Ease:	An extra measurement that is added to ensure comfort or a looser fit.
Notch:	A wedge cut in the pattern or marked on the fabric to indicate matching points.
Pivot:	Support the pattern at a given point, then turn the pattern in a new direction as if on a pivot. This facilitates closing the darts or adding fullness to the pattern along a given edge.
Placket:	A garment opening that fastens with a zip or buttons.
Perpendicular:	A vertical line at a right angle to a horizontal line.
Slash:	A cut or slit made in a pattern to facilitate a construction. When slashing, make sure you stop cutting just before the end of your mark so that all the pieces remain attached. This will guarantee accuracy in further construction.
Square a line:	Draw a line at right angles to the given line, using a set square (i.e. at 90 degrees to the given line).
'Stitch in the ditch':	Stitch in the seam line to minimise time-consuming hand tacking.

index

ILLUSTRATED PAGES IN **BOLD**